THE BIG WEDDING:

**9/11, THE WHISTLE-BLOWERS,
AND THE COVER-UP**

SANDER HICKS

VOX POP#2
2005

The Big Wedding:
9/11, The Whistle-Blowers, and the Cover-Up
© 2005 Sander Hicks

ISBN: 0-9752763-1-X

Vox Pop #1
First Edition, First Printing
July 2005
Printed in the USA, at United Graphics, Inc.

Index by Alexis Wichowski
Copy Editing by Rebecca DeRosa, Larry Eldridge, Melissa Johnson,
& Louisa McMurray

Front Cover: From top left to right:
Sander Hicks, Randy Glass, Daniel Hopsicker and Delmart Vreeland
This photo of Randy Glass is © Rick McKay/The Palm Beach Post. Used
by permission.
Bottom Row: Mohamed Atta, R.G. Abbas of Pakistani ISI, Richard Ben-
Veniste, President George W. Bush and Saudi Crown Prince Abdullah
bin Abdel Aziz

Vox Pop is a Project of the Drench Kiss Media Corporation
Vox Pop/DKMC is distributed to the trade by SCB Distributors.

Come Visit Vox Pop's coffeehouse/bookstore/Instabook printing house at
1022 Cortelyou Road
Brooklyn, NY 11218-5302

VOXPOPNET.NET

For Jim Hatfield
In Solidarity

Now the sneaking serpent walks
In mild humility.
And the just man rages in the wilds
Where lions roam.

—William Blake
The Marriage of Heaven and Hell

A NOTE ON NOTES

To make references immediate and transparent, we used footnotes, set on the same page. For a small number of more minor references, we used End Notes, in lowercase roman numerals, listed on page 162.

TABLE OF CONTENTS

ANTHONY LAPPÉ is executive editor of the Guerrilla News Network's website, GNN.tv. He is a co-author of GNN's *True Lies* (Plume) and the producer of their award-winning Showtime documentary about Iraq, "BattleGround: 21 Days on the Empire's Edge." He has written for more than twenty magazines and news-papers including *Details,* the *New York Times, New York* and *Salon.*

The Big Wedding:

GONZO WE CAN USE

FOREWORD BY ANTHONY LAPPÉ

The call came around 1:30 in the morning. It was Sander on a cell phone from Canada. "Someone wants to talk to you," he said. It was Lt. Delmart "Mike" Vreeland, the notorious self-proclaimed U.S. spy who says he tried to warn the world about 9/11 while sitting in a Canadian jail cell in August 2001. Vreeland had become the epicenter of a raging Internet debate among the legions of wired conspiracy aficionados. Was Vreeland really a spy who tried to warn the world about 9/11, or simply a con man, or some combination of both? The flame wars were hot enough to cook bacon. Sander and I dove headfirst into the controversy in an attempt to separate reality from fantasy in a story in which facts, disinformation, and delusion intersected in a combustible brew. Actually, it was Sander who did most of the diving. I was sitting comfortably at my desk in downtown Manhattan admiring the Empire State Building out my window.

It was August 2002, and Vreeland invited Sander to join him for a weekend get-away in Ontario's lake country with a seventeen-year-old kid Vreeland called his "son," who was clearly *not* his son.

So Sander loaded up his punk rock van and headed out from New York's Long Island toward the Canadian border. I promised him gas money and a 24-hour editorial advice hotline—as editor of the Guerrilla News Network's fledgling website, it was all I had to offer.

The voice on the other end of the late night phone was clearly drunk. Vreeland launched into a rambling monologue about secret messages, attempted hits, and codenames straight out of a Robert Ludlum novel. I explained to him that if he wanted a story that would silence his critics, he would have to focus: We needed tangible evidence that we could check against other sources. After about forty-five intermediately coherent minutes, the lieutenant began babbling about a Star Wars satellite he claimed he had designed for the American government. He explained that if I sent him five hundred dollars—immediately—he could build me a scale model.

"Thanks, but no thanks. GNN doesn't have a satellite model budget," I told him. "Put Sander on the phone."

"Sander, what the fuck is he talking about?" I asked.

"Uh, I'm not sure," was the answer. Hicks and I would find that Mike Vreeland was one of the most exasperating subjects you could ever write about. He was a liar, a sexual deviant, a drug addict and drunk, and most likely, at least partially clinically insane. But as anyone who knows anything about covert ops, none of that meant he *didn't* work for the government. As Hicks would discover, if Vreeland wasn't a spy, he sure had a lot of experienced attorneys, arms dealers, and former intelligence officers believing he was.

Over the course of his investigation, Hicks would uncover some rather startling evidence. He was the first to obtain a signed letter from a respected international lawyer who claimed Vreeland knew certain code words that indicated he had a high national security clearance. Sander also got a hold of Vreeland's official military records, which showed he achieved the rank of lieutenant in the U.S. Navy after serving only five months. The rest of his personal information, showed up suspiciously blank, prompting a Navy records official to suggest that he might be a "low-key type field" or got his rank through unusual means. "You're a fishy guy, sir," said the official. "I don't know if I wanna tell you my name now."

Hicks's reporting clearly proved that Vreeland was involved... with *what*, and *on what level*, I still can't say with any degree of certainty. But I did learn this for a fact: Sander Hicks is a new breed of journalist—a true gonzo investigator who isn't afraid to go where most reporters dare not tread for fear of getting their hands—and reputations—soiled by something as unclean as the dirty truth.

Many have made the connection between Hicks's engaging first-person "extreme" reporting style and the godfather of gonzo—the late, great Hunter S. Thompson. Indeed, Thompson (R.I.P.) was fearless and a true enemy of the powerful and corrupt. But frankly, he made shit up. He never actually "investigated" anything. He simply hung out with dubious characters in bizarre scenarios, and then let the ether do the legwork. It's no surprise that in the end Thompson became a parody of himself—an irrelevant relic in a world that had become too complex, and far too dangerous, for his brand of drug-fueled truth-divining.

Hicks is gonzo we can use. Imagine Henry Rollins meets the young Bob Woodward-a clean-cut, hard-as-nails punk with the reporting chops to take on an empire. Hicks is out to do nothing less than expose the planet's most insidious nexus: the jihadists, bankers, mercenaries, drug dealers, and so-called leaders who are currently pantomiming their way through a charade they've dubbed the "war on terror."

Hicks is no 'net jockey. He offers up real, boots-on-the-ground, face-to-face reporting backed up with informed analysis. He's a man on a mission, and you're along for the ride.

That is what sets this book apart.

The towers were still standing when skeptics first began to question the official 9/11 narrative. It soon blossomed into an international cottage industry of 9/11 truth seekers. There was much to ponder: How the most powerful nation in the world could let itself be so vulnerable to a home-grown attack; how the President could continue to read a book about goats after being told the nation was at war; how a terrorist's intact passport just happened to survive the fireball to be found on the street in lower Manhattan; how the FBI could show up at the Florida flight school of the lead hijackers that afternoon if they weren't already on their tails; how a bunch of barely competent student pilots could so expertly execute their attacks, including a spectacular spiral dive—dropping seven thousand feet and turning 270 degrees in about 2.5 minutes—over the nation's capital that ended an approach that nearly trimmed the grass of the Pentagon lawn.

Over the course of the last four years, the so-called "9/11 Truth Movement" has become a model of open-source citizen participation, engaging people from all walks of life from around the world in an inspiring collective search for the truth. But it has always been plagued by a glaring contradiction: it has relied almost exclusively on the reporting of mainstream news sources at the same time it rails against the mainstream press as players in the grand cover-up. But by far, the most troubling aspect of this fledgling movement lurks on its fringes. Thousands of hours are spent debating theories that defy rational thought and mounds of physical evidence. The planes were fakes! The passengers had been let off at a secret location, and drone planes flew into the towers. No, the planes were actually missiles! See look at the "pods" on the bottom of these blurry video stills. It was been nearly impossible for the responsible members of the movement to distance themselves from the lunacy.

Anonymous characters popped up with names like "Web Fairy," and were taken seriously by thousands of seemingly intelligent people. A bizarre alternative universe emerged in which the more outlandish the claim, the more it was taken as gospel. Those who questioned the podpeople and their equivalents, were dubbed government stooges. It was farce that took on aspects of magical realism—a fantasy world which one day will quite possibly be exposed as a deliberate disinformation program designed to taint the dedicated seekers of truth as paranoid "conspiracy theorists."

The Big Wedding builds on the best the 9/11 research community has to offer, while breaking important new ground. Hicks presents startling new evidence indicating that the Bush administration had detailed foreknowledge of 9/11 and did nothing to stop it—or was up to something much more sinister. Hicks obtains shocking revelations from government whistle-blowers and top researchers, including former FBI/ATF informant Randy Glass. Hicks looks at precedents and evidence that suggest the unthinkable: the 9/11 attack was an inside job.

Randy Glass has already been a subject of everyone from NBC to Paul Thompson's *Terror Timeline* encyclopedia on 9/11. But Hicks goes further. We learn that the FBI informant personally warned former Senator Bob Graham (D-FL) about the impending attacks in a face-to-face meeting in the summer of 2001. Glass tells Hicks of a dinner meeting with Pakistani spies in New York's swanky Tribeca Grill in which the Al Qaeda-connected operative casually mentions the nearby Twin Towers won't be standing for long. Glass tells Hicks U.S. State Department officials told him in July 2001, "Don't go to the media" and, "We know all about planes being flown into the World Trade Center." The CIA seemed to have plenty to say about 9/11 just weeks before, when President Bush was handed a Presidential Daily Brief entitled "Bin Laden Determined to Strike in U.S."

Glass is just one of the rogue's gallery of ex-spies, ex-criminals, and whistle-blowers you'll meet in *The Big Wedding*.

Many historians and guerrilla journalists have already raised an eyebrow at the Pakistani ISI's connection to the CIA. Hicks goes further, tying in the notorious BCCI, the Bank of Credit and Commerce International. Many have written about ISI's relationship to the Taliban and Al Qaeda. Hicks explores the little-known, but much more established Muslim Brotherhood, an organization with historical ties to the Third Reich. And for those of us shocked at the Bush administration's willingness to fabricate evidence to justify wars, Hicks goes back to 1976 and finds Cheney and Rumsfeld high up in the Ford White House, fabricating reality through a group called "Team B." When the CIA wouldn't justify an inflated Soviet threat, and legitimate massive defense spending, Team B was created to do just that. Hicks also provides a detailed and enlightening analysis of the latest neo-con carnival, the Project for the New American Century.

The Big Wedding may not make Hicks many friends on the fringes of 9/11 "truth movement," nor is it likely his white-hot revelations will find much space in the mainstream press, which has proven incapable, or simply unwilling, to investigate even the most obvious contradictions in the government's story.

Ultimately, it's for you to decide whether Hicks in on to something big in *The Big Wedding*. I'll simply kick you off with this anecdote:

Shortly after Hicks's Vreeland story ran on GNN's website, a family friend—a lifelong CIA officer—contacted him. They talked about what Hicks had found. He casually inquired if Hicks had ever had any interest in working for the Company.

The friend said Hicks had some skills they could put to use. Hicks declined the offer. He's a guerilla operative for the people, not the secret elite. In *The Big Wedding*, he's handing in his preliminary field report.

The Big Wedding:

AUTHOR'S INTRODUCTION

There is a specter haunting America. A faded but persistent truth has been repressed. There is a story about power that needs to be told.

From 1999 to 2001, I was the publisher of Jim Hatfield's *Fortunate Son: George W. Bush and the Making of an American President.* The book was the first George W. Bush bio on the market. It was also the first and only Bush book to report the connection between the Bush and bin Laden families, or Bush's long-rumored early '70s cocaine arrest. During the 2000 presidential campaign, *Fortunate Son* was the only book published that was critical of George W. Bush. The book was fair, but it was aggressive. Also, author Jim Hatfield had some skeletons of his own in his own closet; consequently, both Jim and I went through a roller coaster ride in the media. It became evident that it's difficult for a writer to tell the whole truth about the Bush family. If you call it as you see it in this world, you have a rare courage.

Jim had been in and out of jail since he was eighteen. In Arkansas, during his early twenties, he wrote bad checks, committed minor burglaries, and once stole a car. During the '80s, he got in with the wrong crowd in Dallas, and was arrested for his role in his boss's alleged plan to murder his mistress (his boss ran a finance and real estate company and prided himself on connections to some powerful players). Hatfield did five years in Huntsville—"the Walls," as it's called, because of the gigantic thirty-foot high stone walls ringing the facility.

Other books published that year about George W. Bush—namely, *W: Revenge of the Bush Dynasty* by Elizabeth Mitchell and *Favorite Son* by Bill Minutaglio didn't examine a certain fact: Bush's first oil company was funded by the family of Osama bin Laden, who in 1998 was involved in the bombing of U.S. embassies in Africa. Hatfield had ambition and an acute nose for scandal. He emphasized the bin Laden connection. I asked Hatfield his source on this. If it was well-sourced, I felt sure it would be recognized as a startling anomaly to be tackled properly by the top journalists over at "60 Minutes" where we were due to arrive soon. Hatfield instantly responded that the Bush/bin Laden material was solid. Two award-winning reporters for *Time* had covered the Bank of Credit and Commerce International (BCCI) scandal, and their book, *The Outlaw Bank*, detailed the Bush/bin Laden connection. The book's first-hand witness, Bill White, had been in business for many years with James Bath in Texas. Bath and George W. Bush were flying buddies from the Texas Air National Guard throughout the early '70s. Bath bragged that he worked for the CIA. He was proud to tell Bill White that he had worked with Bush Sr. and some serious Saudi heavyweights: Sheikh Khalid bin Mahfouz and Salem bin Laden.

The Bush/bin Laden material never made it on the air at "60 Minutes." Also unaired was Hatfield's breakthrough research on the 1972 Bush cocaine arrest. (This arrest story should have shut down the Bush Campaign in 1999: young Dubya was busted around the time he and James Bath were simultaneously suspended from flying in the Guard. The arrest helps explain why Bush went AWOL from the Texas Air National Guard at this time.) Instead, "60 Minutes" focused on Hatfield's own skeletons. The segment's producer, Jay Kernis, led me to believe that he'd treat us fairly on air. I later asked him why "60 Minutes" ignored the content of Jim's book. Jay snapped at me, "It's not the *media's* job to be *critical!*"

After "60 Minutes" was broadcast, Jim and I were sued by Hatfield's ex-boss Larry Burk and Delores Kay Burrow, his former co-worker. Burk and Burrow took issue with the new foreword. This foreword was supposed to be a response to the information exposed about Jim, the stuff that people were focusing on. Lawyers for Burk and Burrow called me up and implied they wouldn't need evidence to prove Jim's story was wrong and defamatory. They didn't claim to have any evidence that would prove Larry Burk did not ask Jim Hatfield to pass money to a hit man to take out a woman Burk claimed was bribing him. Instead, the lawyers claimed their major evidence was that Jim looked sketchy on "60 Minutes."

Their lawsuit disrupted my independent publishing company, Soft Skull Press, Inc. and almost choked the life out of it completely. When the national distributor of *Fortunate Son*, Consortium, tucked tail and ran, we were stuck with a warehouse full of books. We had printed forty-five thousand. Consortium had sold about thirty thousand into the trade. When my company got sued, Consortium decided they could no longer distribute the book, although they had an exclusive contractual obligation to sell to the North American book trade. Because of that decision, we were unable to sell any books through normal channels for the rest of the campaign season. After "60 Minutes", we could only watch as most of the thirty thousand sales were returned by wholesalers back to Consortium's warehouse. However, thanks to our website, which sold the book directly to the public, we were able to hold on.

Jim Hatfield wasn't doing so well. He lost two other book contracts. He got trashed in a big breathy feature on the front cover of the *Washington Post* "Style" section and in the now-defunct haute media criticism journal *Brill's Content*, among others. Certain inaccurate statements about Jim's past became so commonplace in the media, most reporters repeated them. Because of the spread of these inaccuracies, Jim's reputation was annihilated.

We did get one solid break together from "Crier Today" on Court TV. Former Texas Judge Catherine Crier dealt with the topic of Hatfield's past in a succinct and non-sensational manner, and then got to the meat of the topic: Bush's SEC investigation, the big oil connections, and the abysmal record on the environment. But Jim Hatfield never bounced back from the "60 Minutes" deathblow in early February 2000. His self-respect had been continually trashed since October 1999, when the *Dallas Morning News* broke a story about Hatfield's past. Bush family lawyers started threatening lawsuits, and St. Martin's Press caved in right away and recalled his book from stores. St. Martin's trade division president Sally Richardson told the *New York Times* that the one hundred thousand books they had printed would now be burned. "They're heat, furnace fodder!" she told the October 23, 1999 *Times*, who put it on page A12. (This is the article that originally inspired me to look into reprinting the book.)

Four days earlier, Jacob Weisberg published a piece in Slate[1]

1   Published by Slate.com, Tuesday, Oct. 19, 1999
http://slate.msn.com/id/1003850/

titled "Busting Bush's Biographer" that claimed the sources on the Bush cocaine arrest story didn't sound authentic to him. Without evidence, Weisberg presented his opinion as news. This pattern was typical of almost all aboveground reporting on Hatfield in the fall of 1999. The Bush cocaine arrest story had been inside a set of "long-rumored allegations" that only Jim purported to have "nailed" according to the *Washington Post.*[2] But in a response typical of most reporters, Pete Slover of the *Dallas Morning News* admitted later to a film crew that his hackles, or at least his radar, went up when this rumor became published.[3] When Hatfield came up to shoot "60 Minutes" he took me aside on a street corner and quietly said that his sources on the Bush cocaine arrest story were Karl Rove, Clay Johnson, and Bush's minister, James Mayfield. So, how did Hatfield get access to Bush campaign insiders? Where did he get the private phone numbers for Bush-brain Rove and Bush's lifelong friend/aide Clay Johnson?

Clay Johnson was a Dallas businessman in the '80s who ran a big mail order business. Jim told me that Johnson was a friendly Dallas business associate of Larry Burk and Kay Burrow's. In 1988, when the sensational car bomb story hit the papers, it is likely that Johnson heard about it. The story was in the headlines and the ATF arrived to investigate. When Bush cocaine arrest rumors started flying around in August '99 (originally on Salon.com, thanks to anonymous sources[4]), the Bush campaign needed a way to kill the story. James Carville and Karl Rove favored the same technique: Get out ahead of the media by at least two or three moves and break the story before it breaks you. Simultaneous with the cocaine arrest rumors in August '99, Rove had this nosy biographer Jim Hatfield calling the campaign all the time asking pesky questions about Bush's background with the oil companies and how Bush dodged Vietnam. It's likely that Clay Johnson would have informed Rove about Hatfield's Texas felonies. A perfect opportunity to distract the media away from Bush's antics in 1972 fell into their laps. (In 2004, something very similar happened to distract everyone from Bush's spotty career in 1972. This time, it ended the career of CBS News's Dan Rather.)

When Bush took the White House, a lot of folks joked, "oh well, at least it's good for your book business, har har." But in my

2 As per *Washington Post,* March 19, 2000, in a story titled "Unfortunate Son" by Kathy Sawyer
3 "Horns and Halos" directed by Michael Galinsky and Suki Hawley (2002) The film accurately depicts Hatfield, Bush and me, warts and all, and our efforts to republish *Fortunate Son.* Despite good reviews, after 9/11 the film was not able to get a full theatrical release.
4 "Bush Up to his Arse in Allegations! Sharp-Tooth E-mail, Killer Bees, and Bags of Worms. Will This Hound Hunt?" by Amy Reiter, *Salon,* August 25, 1999

The Big Wedding:

gut I had a feeling it was going to be actually very bad for business.

I convinced Jim to come to Chicago to the BookExpo in June 2001. We had a new edition of the book, and a new distributor. We called a press conference. With Hatfield by my side, I revealed the names of his three sources on the Bush cocaine arrest. We left Chicago elated. After all, the *Washington Post, USA Today,* and Reuters had all been there. We never suspected none of them would write about it.

A month and a half later, Jim Hatfield was dead. On July 17, 2001, he checked into a Days Inn thirty miles outside his hometown of Bentonville, Arkansas and some time that night, overdosed on prescription narcotics and vodka. He left a four-page suicide note. He loved his family and said that in his final written words. "Blame it on FS," he wrote, using our in-house abbreviation for the book.

After he was dead, I was shown financial records that seemed to indicate that Jim had been pulling a credit card scam since April. If those records are true, he was trying to pull off an amateur's con. I'd like to think he was smarter than applying for a business credit card using his former cellmate's name. But Hatfield always was a better writer than he was a criminal. His note included the language: "It's been all downhill since Oct. '99 and this day was my destiny...just remember, no matter what anyone tells you, I was a good man who got caught up in bad circumstances."

I took a leave of absence from my publishing company. I moved out of the Lower East Side of New York City on the 10th of September 2001. I moved everything I owned in one load and returned the rented truck to Manhattan late that night. I remember an eerie stillness in the city. I felt so tender about Manhattan. I still wasn't sure if moving out to my aunt's place in Long Island for a little while was the right decision. I needed to take some time off, get some space from the whole tragedy. Make sure I was still alive. Go to Arkansas and make sure Jim's death was really a suicide.

The next morning, my aunt found me in her backyard, reading a book. "There's been a horrible disaster. Both World Trade towers are down." I thought she was exaggerating. We turned on her TV and were subjected to the traumatizing effects of the same repetitive images: the plane breaking the membrane of the building like a knife stabbing through paper. The 24-hour news channels right away were blaming Osama bin Laden (although no one actually took responsibility until seven months later).

From that point on I began to see the spirit of Jim Hatfield everywhere. As I traveled the country to meet witnesses and informants, men used up and discarded by covert ops, there were stark similarities to him in rejected, freelance mavericks: Delmart Vreeland, Randy Glass, Daniel Hopsicker, and many other whistle-blowers. Jim knows these guys: he was one of them. He had worked in the "go-go '80s" Dallas real estate world with people like them. He had done time with people like them. These men all had damaged reputations and had to work twice as hard to get people to listen to them. And most of the time, they were ignored by a media inclined to believe government spokesmen.

There's a consistency to the story that these whistle-blowers tell here in *The Big Wedding*. Through Randy Glass and Delmart Vreeland, we'll hear about a high degree of 9/11 fore-knowledge on the part of the military/intelligence complex. Through Daniel Hopsicker, we'll gain insights into who Mohamed Atta associated with, why he trained at an airstrip with a history of military/intelligence intrigue, and what his motivations really were. By studying Team B and The Project for a New American Century, we learn that the same men who flouted the law in the Iran/Contra/BCCI scandal stated outright throughout the '90s that they now needed a "cataclysmic event" in order to motivate the people to support wars for U.S. world domination. And we'll meet the loosely organized national grassroots movement that uses truth and networked intelligence to wage an info-war of resistance.

This book is a history from below, built on the cornerstone of the eyewitness testimony of working-class spies, researchers and witnesses. I add my own research into Muslim Brotherhood, the CIA/ISI[5] client relationship, the history of BCCI, and how all these things are the tools of an ascending neoconservative agenda. Any virtuous student of history can see it plainly.

I wrote this book because I admire the info-war street fighters who have everything to lose by talking about their experiences: Vreeland, Glass, and Hopsicker have all received death threats for their work. They speak out anyway. Meanwhile, the ruling class strategists have everything to lose by their real histories being reported. Fortunately for them, it seldom is in a cynical, disoriented, glossy, corporate-controlled, advertising-oriented, professional media. But once we begin an awakening to what's really at the heart of current events, the Spirit of History will emerge in the will of the people and the whole charade will soon be over.

---

5   ISI is the CIA of Pakistan, it stands for "Inter-Services Intelligence." BCCI is the Bank of Credit and Commerce International, which we learn more about in Chapter 2.

In the last years of his life, Jim Hatfield was fond of quoting poet Langston Hughes, "I've been insulted, eliminated, locked in, locked out, and left holding the bag. But I am still here." Anytime someone stands up and tells the truth about the Bush family, or 9/11, Jim Hatfield and all the fallen truth tellers of history are once again, still here.

The Big Wedding:

CHAPTER ONE

"THE JEWISH JOE PESCI" RANDY GLASS AND THE PAKISTANI CONNECTION

Allan Duncan was a New Jersey social worker until 2004, when budget cuts slashed away his job. He blamed Bush. The cutting of social services gave Allan more time for his hobby: broadcasting the best 9/11 news stories to his sizable email list.

On June 15, 2004, I received a personal email from Allan, with the subject line "Very Important Message." I had been working at "INN World Report," a TV news show on Dish Network's "Free Speech TV." Allan had someone very hot for us to talk to: Randy Glass, the jewelry con man who had turned into a major FBI/ATF informant for something called, "Operation Diamondback." Diamondback had infiltrated terrorist groups interested in buying large quantities of lethal weapons. "Dateline NBC" had done two pieces already on Glass but in Allan's view, those pieces "never revealed the really blockbuster 9/11 stuff he had."

Allan breathlessly wrote: "Several months ago, Glass had his cover blown by the FBI, and was held in a hotel for five weeks for his own safety...The FBI has been trying to gag him and has threatened to have his probation violated and thrown in prison and charged with obstruction of justice if he talks to the press. We had interviews set up with Sy Hersh and *Vanity Fair* and they both fell through because of threats to Randy."

I had serious respect for Seymour Hersh of the *New Yorker*. I had recently posted a little tribute to his investigative reporting of the "web of lies" at the White House on my home page. Who knew why Sy Hersh had passed on the story—I had to do it.

Glass, according to Allan, was now willing to talk. "He has now been cut loose by the FBI and is back home and in fear of his life."

I had read about Glass already in the "9/11 Timeline" published online by Paul Thompson and Cooperative Research. It was a memorable story: at a dinner in June 1999, at the Tribeca Grill, Glass was wining and dining Rajaa Gulum Abbas, a Pakistani arms dealer, and his friends. Glass and ATF agent Dick Stoltz were posing as weapons brokers, as part of a federal sting operation. Abbas had close connections to the Pakistani intelligence elite, the ISI. In fact, Glass later told me Abbas had identified as an ISI agent.

The tony Tribeca Grill, owned by Robert De Niro, was just north of the World Trade Center in 1999. Abbas boasted to his dinner companions that he wouldn't have any problem taking out the entire downtown restaurant, "Because it's full of Americans."

Toward the end of the meal, he gestured out toward the Twin Towers, and stated, "Those towers are coming down."

Although Glass told this part of the story to "Dateline NBC," it was kept off the record by the FBI. Like most of the other juicy details, it wasn't broadcast. Glass at the time was prevented by his FBI/ATF handlers from talking about "an ongoing investigation" on camera. The real meat of the story was broken by the *Palm Beach Post,* on October 17, 2002, in a story by crackerjack reporter John Pacenti.

In July and August 2001, just before Glass started to serve a seven-month sentence for a $6 million jewelry scam, he reached out to Senator Bob Graham and U.S. Rep. Robert Wexler. He said he told staffers for both lawmakers that Pakistani operative R.G. Abbas, working for the Taliban, made three references to imminent plans to attack the World Trade Center during the probe, which ended in June 2001. He described the meeting caught on tape at the Tribeca Grill, during which Abbas had declared that the World Trade Center towers "are coming down."

"Dateline" used Glass in a follow-up piece five months later, but the crucial details about R.G. Abbas remained unreported.

But now in July 2004, Randy Glass was eager to go on record. And I was eager to get him on "INN World Report," to scoop "Dateline." R.G. Abbas and the ISI for whom he worked had their paw prints all over 9/11. The *Times of India* and French news agency AFP reported that the head of ISI, General Mahmood, wired one hundred thousand dollars to Mohamed

Atta, through Saeed Sheikh, right before 9/11. (I will examine this incident, and its cover-up in the next chapter.) The CIA and the ISI have been joined in a hellish marriage of convenience spawned by Afghanistan's Mujahedeen/Soviet civil war. As we'll see in the next chapter, the results of this have been monstrous children: BCCI, the Taliban and Al Qaeda.

In preparation for my interview, I had Randy overnight us copies of the "Dateline" shows. I was actually pretty impressed. Unlike a lot of network news shows, these were relatively gutsy. They played tapes Randy had made of Egyptian/U.S. arms dealer Diaa Mohsen talking like Don Corleone, explaining in nervous barks of laughter that his friends the Pakistanis were in cahoots with "the Taliban from Afghanistan" and "Osama bin Laden." On surveillance videotape, Mohsen and Abbas walk into a warehouse and look at Stinger missiles. Glass is alongside them, playing the part of the wise guy to the hilt. He later told me, "I'm an adrenaline junkie. I love the action."

Diaa Mohsen, according to Glass, was a "lunatic capable of killing anybody, anytime, anywhere, period. And he has, like, Manson-type followers. Believe me, you have no idea. I've met them, I know." Mohsen is kind of an anti-celebrity in his native Egypt, being a former member of the Egyptian National Soccer Team and an Olympic long jumper. On "Dateline," Glass asks him, "How do you travel to all of these places without coming up on the radar screen of the CIA or other intelligence agencies in the world? This doesn't make sense to me." Mohsen explained that, courtesy of friends at the Venezuelan Embassy, he enjoyed owning a "special passport." Mohsen claimed he could, "enter any fucking country and be protected."

In the August '02 "Dateline" story, Mohsen and the Pakistanis don't just want anti-aircraft missiles, they want the hard stuff: "heavy water," a.k.a. "sweet water." That would be an order for Deuterium Oxide, which is water, H_2O, but with scrambled hydrogen isotopes. Heavy water can turn natural uranium into plutonium. It's the garage way to make a thermonuclear bomb: you bypass having to enrich the uranium. Heavy water is what Nazi Germany was trying to use toward the end of World War II. And it's the method the Pakistanis wanted to use, with Glass and Mohsen's supply run.

Heavy water was the deal breaker. Glass promised Mohsen they could find some.

According to "Dateline," the deal fell apart when $32 million failed to materialize from the Pakistanis. (Although, according to Glass, the $32 million was wired over, but the Feds "bounced it back" in order to not embarrass the Pakistani government, and directly link them to terrorism.)

On June 12, 2001, Diaa Mohsen and "Mike" Malik (their connection in New Jersey) were arrested, along with their Wall Street money launderer, Kevin Ingram. According to sealed court records, at the time of their arrest, Malik and Mohsen were charged with "money laundering, violation of the Arms Export Control Act, Title 21 844(d), obtaining explosives to kill or injure someone, and Title 18 Section 371, conspiracy to commit all those offenses." Yet Malik did zero time inside, and walked free on a million dollar bond. His partner, nuclear weapons/death broker Diaa Mohsen, got sentenced to a cool thirty months in prison. "The whole thing was a fix," Glass says today.

Mohsen's light sentence was allegedly the result of his helping the U.S. Government find other terrorist-linked individuals. But Mike Malik's attorney James Eisenberg cryptically implied that the special connections in this case would make a big difference at sentencing time. He told *Talk* magazine Kevin "Ingram's got information on more than just the clients in this case."[6]

(l. to r.) Kevin Ingram, Randy Glass, and Diaa Mohsen

Looks like that "information" did the trick. Ingram was sentenced to a slim eighteen months. In a cruel twist, the harshest sentence in the case was reserved for Walter Kapij, Ingram's hired pilot. Kapij was only peripherally involved, but not quite as well-connected. As the terrorist arms dealers and the Wall Street playboy money man cut deals, Kapij got sent away thirty-three months.

The ATF's undercover agent Dick Stoltz told "Dateline," "Quite frankly, I was always wondering when maybe the case would be taken away from ATF." They asked if he meant FBI or CIA. "FBI at the minimum," said Stoltz.

This is similar to what "Dateline" producer Richard Greenberg told me, as I prepared our segment on Glass at INN. He expressed surprise that the *New York Times*, or at least New Jersey's *Bergen County Record*, didn't cover this breaking story. But then, Greenberg should understand the media's behavior: he himself was extremely careful about what parts of Glass's story he was willing to report. Not including the crucial "those

6   For more on Ingram, see "Wall Street's Solider of Fortune" by Leah Nathan Spiro (November 2001). Published in the now-defunct *Talk* magazine, it is available online.

The Big Wedding:

towers are coming down" from Abbas in either broadcast was a curious omission. It's one thing to bypass it during an "ongoing investigation," but it's especially curious that Greenberg then did related follow-up stories that also left out evidence of FBI foreknowledge of 9/11. Greenberg (and the mainstream newspapers that didn't report his stories) seem to be deliberately treading lightly around an established CIA/ISI client relationship.

Although crucial details were left out by "Dateline," their segment ends with this jejune comment: "For his part, Randy Glass says there's a lot more on those tapes, leads the government could pursue, people still out there only too happy to supply weapons to the network of terror."

Read between the lines. Discard the naïve tone, and what "Dateline" really said here was: "There's a lot more on those tapes, leads we could have pursued. However, we didn't do so, because the government has made it obvious that punishing CIA-connected Pakistanis and Egyptians is the last thing they are going to do."

The Randy Glass story exposes just how important the Pakistani connection is to understanding 9/11. The story was brought to millions of people by NBC, who in turn showed how self-censoring the media is on topics related to 9/11. All evidence points to the fact that Pakistani intelligence agents were in the U.S. buying nuclear and conventional weapons for the Taliban and the 9/11 attack. When the government failed to properly investigate and prosecute the guilty, NBC was content to shrug and say "there's a lot more on those tapes."

CIA intrigue and FBI malfeasance around 9/11 has thus far been dismissed as "incompetence" in the mainstream media. But if "incompetence" was at fault, then someone would have been fired or demoted after 9/11. Just the opposite happened at FBI, and throughout the military/intelligence complex. For example, David Frasca, head of the Radical Fundamentalist Unit at FBI, ignored or suppressed warnings from the FBI's Ken Williams, Coleen Rowley, and Randy Glass. However, after 9/11, instead of being held responsible, he was promoted to number three in charge of domestic terrorism at the FBI.

The more we understand the U.S./Pakistani relationship, the history of the relationship of the CIA and the Pakistani ISI, or the CIA and FBI's cultivation and use of Egyptian double agents since before the 1993 World Trade Center bombing, the more we understand how and why 9/11 happened. Once we meet whistle-blowers like Randy Glass, we begin to realize that each of them had a specific kind of foreknowledge of 9/11.

In the case of Randy Glass, he got really lucky. His credibility and public persona received crucially important good first impressions, thanks to a largely amicable, if selective, treatment at the hands of "Dateline." If producer Richard Greenberg had been a cynical sort, he easily could have turned on the former jewelry thief. Instead, he took a cue from the court records, where many voices inside the FBI and ATF spoke of Glass's gusto and valor.[7]

JULY 2, 2004:

WE BROADCAST THE RANDY GLASS STORY

So, after watching "Dateline's" work, it was up to us to surpass it. We broadcast our Glass story, and it included the television debut of the R.G. Abbas prediction of 9/11. Here's a transcript of how our on-screen interview with Randy Glass went. This is a verbatim transcript, minus a few edits for space.

A still from the INN World Report Randy Glass story.

Originally Broadcast: 7/2/04 by "INN World Report," Free Speech TV, Dish Network

INN HOST MIZAN KIRBY-NUNES:

In an INN special report, Sander Hicks interviews 9/11 whistle-blower and former undercover agent, Randy Glass.

SANDER HICKS: Randy Glass, welcome to "INN World Report."

RANDY GLASS: Thank you.

SANDER HICKS: It's good to have you with us. You were a diamonds broker, a con man, and a convicted felon, but in the late 90s you became an informant for the FBI and ATF. You worked under deep cover tracking terrorists by posing as an arms dealer. Randy, let's start by talking about two real arms dealers, Mike Malik and Diaa Mohsen.

RANDY GLASS: Yes. Basically it started out with Diaa Mohsen. Diaa Mohsen introduced me to several different terrorists groups. Throughout the thirty-one-month investigation, I had four different terrorists groups in my home where my family lived. That was to create a feeling of comfort and credibility. But to really give the credibility, the government had set me up with a weapons warehouse, because words only go so far. So, once we qualified the buyers, we would take them—"we" meaning myself and an undercover federal

7   According to sealed court records, FBI Agent Steve Burdelski testified that Glass "traveled to Trinidad to arrest a fugitive. He's put himself in harm's way. He's been good to work with, he's been reliable, and he's eager to assist law enforcement."

agent, Dick Stoltz—we would take them to our weapons warehouse, where we showed them a multitude of sophisticated weapon systems, up to and including nuclear material.

SANDER HICKS: Right. These guys were interested in whatever and whenever you could supply them with.

RANDY GLASS: That's correct.

SANDER HICKS: Why don't we play a tape? You have an audiotape that will prove that you worked with these terrorists.

RANDY GLASS: Yes, this is Diaa Mohsen, and he is sitting with Mohamed Malik, and this was the first time that I had met Malik over the phone.

[audio clip]

RANDY GLASS: What are they looking to buy?

DIAA MOHSEN: Every fucking thing. Whatever we have-

RANDY GLASS: They got money? You know these people?

DIAA MOHSEN: ...can't mention the fucking dummy's name on the phone.

RANDY GLASS: Well...all of a sudden, right, you're not going to talk on this phone. This—

DIAA MOHSEN: All right, OK.

RANDY GLASS: OK, huh?

DIAA MOHSEN: You know who's supplying those guns?

RANDY GLASS: Who? Yeah-

DIAA MOHSEN: Osama bin Laden

RANDY GLASS: That's very nice.

DIAA MOHSEN: Yeah. [Laughter]

RANDY GLASS: There's [indistinct] OK.

DIAA MOHSEN: [Laughter]

RANDY GLASS: All right, who—what's—

DIAA MOHSEN: Do they have money?

RANDY GLASS: What is the name of this group?

DIAA MOHSEN: The Taliban from Afghanistan.

[End of clip]

SANDER HICKS: These people connected you to a different arms buyer named Abbas.

RANDY GLASS: That's correct.

SANDER HICKS: ...And I know that this led to a meeting that you have talked about to me earlier, in the Tribeca Grill.... What happened at that meeting?

RANDY GLASS: ...I met with— well, first of all, I flew to New York with FBI Agent Steve Burdelski

ISI arms broker & 9/11 intel source R. G. Abbas

and United States Customs Agent William Puff. And I was kept waiting over three hours downstairs in the lobby while I was waiting for them to—we were meeting with the FBI Terrorism Task Force in New York.

...There were about a dozen FBI Terrorism Task Force officials that were at the bar and seated at different tables. I met with Diaa Mohsen, who introduced me to Mohamed Malik and R. G. Abbas. The four of us sat down at a table; I was wired for sound. At that meeting, Abbas was all business. And he inquired about purchasing a shipload of sophisticated weapons systems, such as Stinger missiles, weapons-grade plutonium, nuclear triggers, things like that.

When he asked about the nuclear materials, he asked if it was available, and of course I told him, "Yes, it was," but that I would have to find out more information.

SANDER HICKS: And for people outside of New York, they might not know that the Tribeca Grill is—was—within sightlines of the World Trade Center.

RANDY GLASS: Ah, yes. It's not far at all.

SANDER HICKS: And he, in fact, made a reference to the World Trade Center at that dinner.

RANDY GLASS: Yes, he did. He told me at that dinner that the Towers—and it's a quote: "Those towers are coming down."

SANDER HICKS: Which leads me to my next question. I know that you then, in July of 2001, contacted your senator, Bob Graham in Florida, Congressman Wexler, as well as your personal friend, the state senator there in Florida—

RANDY GLASS: Yes, I did.

SANDER HICKS: And what resulted from those contacts? Those faxes that you faxed them?

RANDY GLASS: Well, let me just—we're skipping way ahead—let me just tell you that this meeting was in July of 1999, OK? So, I think it's very important to note that Abbas, Malik, and Mohsen came to Florida and we had shown—when I say "we," the government had set me up with an arms warehouse.

SANDER HICKS: Right, because it was a sting operation trying to find out who the terrorists were that wanted to buy weapons.

RANDY GLASS: Correct.

SANDER HICKS: And these terrorists were linked to what groups?

RANDY GLASS: To Al Qaeda, the Taliban, Osama bin Laden. But basically...I would have to say...that even the Saudis that pulled off the 9/11 attack...if I were to say that there was a state-sponsored organization, I would say that it was Pakistan and their ISI, which is like their equivalent to our CIA.

SANDER HICKS: So, which of these three guys had links to ISI?

RANDY GLASS: Mohamed Malik and Abbas. Abbas was a high-ranking ISI official.

The Big Wedding:

SANDER HICKS: OK. So this led you to some inside knowledge about 9/11, correct?

RANDY GLASS: Oh, absolutely.

SANDER HICKS: What was your inside knowledge?

RANDY GLASS: OK, the investigation continued on, OK? And Abbas brought—sent—he went back to Pakistan. He and Mohamed Malik got on a plane and flew back to Pakistan.

Malik came back. Abbas sent other operatives from the ISI, including one of their nuclear scientists, associate of their main nuclear scientist, Khan. He sent back one of his associates to inspect weapons-grade plutonium to make sure that it was weapons-grade plutonium, and nuclear triggers. As well as other sophisticated weapons systems.

9/11 was supposed to be a nuclear attack.

SANDER HICKS: July 2001, you knew enough about 9/11—

RANDY GLASS: Yeah.

SANDER HICKS: That you contacted Senator Bob Graham.

RANDY GLASS: Yes.

SANDER HICKS: I have the fax here on my desk...

[Referencing this document:]

You knew enough about the World Trade Center being attacked that you wanted to contact the senator at—who was on the Senate Intelligence Committee and let him know.

RANDY GLASS: Correct. And I did.

SANDER HICKS: What was the result of that?

RANDY GLASS: I was put in touch with one of Senator Graham's workers in his—on his staff. His name was Charles Yonts. And I spoke to Mr. Yonts about a half a dozen times. I provided him with all of the information and material that I had about airplanes being flown into the World Trade Center.

SANDER HICKS: Right. And then I know Kathleen Walters at WPTV/NBC, Channel 5 in Florida, had a very combative interview with Senator Graham.

RANDY GLASS: Correct.

SANDER HICKS: She cornered him at a press conference?

RANDY GLASS: Yes. This was after 9/11.

SANDER HICKS: And we're about to see a tape of that. What can you tell us about this tape?

RANDY GLASS: Well, I can tell you that Senator Graham admitted to Kathleen Walters on that video that I had in fact given him warning before 9/11 about the attack, about airplanes being flown into the World Trade Center.

SANDER HICKS: OK, now that's major. So, on that tape that we're about to see, he effectively admits that you did, in July of 2001, know about 9/11 and notified him, a U.S. senator on the Senate Intelligence Committee.

RANDY GLASS: Yes.

[Interview clip with Kathleen Walters and Senator Graham[ii]]

KATHLEEN WALTERS: "A few months before September 11, your office received information from ATF informant Randy Glass, who was working with the Terrorism Task Force, and he also advised your office of terrorist intentions to bring down the World Trade Center. And this was before September 11...

SENATOR GRAHAM: [nods affirmatively.]

KATHLEEN WALTERS: Your office tells me it forwarded information from Mr. Glass to the Intelligence Committee, and my question is, why did no one from the Committee follow up with Mr. Glass to pursue this?

SENATOR GRAHAM: Well because we in turn gave that information to the appropriate intelligence agency. We are an oversight and legislative agency. The actual operations of collection of information, interviewing possible sources is the responsibility of the FBI if it's a domestic matter, or the CIA if it's foreign.

The Big Wedding:

Kathleen Walters: How serious were...you know, when you heard about Mr. Glass and the information that he had, [he] obviously got a lot of exposure on "Dateline." How big of a concern did you personally have when you heard about this serious information that he had?

Senator Graham: Well, I was concerned about that and a dozen other pieces of information, which were emanating in the summer of 2001, all of which we transmitted to the appropriate intelligence agency. In the report that we issued this week, there were four to five pages of incidents where people were [indistinct] credible to use commercial airliners as weapons of mass destruction by flying them into a building.

So, that was not, or should not have been, a surprise that this was a technique that had the potential of moving from a threat to the reality that it became on September 11th."

[End of audio clip]

Sander Hicks: So, Randy, what's the bottom line about the FBI and their involvement in 9/11?

Randy Glass: OK, I believe that the FBI thwarted the—a full and factual investigation into 9/11. That is my belief based on my experience and observations of how the agents that I worked with handled the information.

Sander Hicks: Well, thanks a lot for being on the program, Randy Glass, former FBI informant.

GOD COMES OUT IN THE DETAILS IN POST-PRODUCTION: RANDY FINGERS THE STATE DEPARTMENT

The show was choppy, but a good start. With the tight deadline, neither Randy nor I felt like we got the chance to do all that we could.

Later that week, I called Randy back to go over some facts so I could write a proper introduction. It was the day of the broadcast, a sunny Friday. We were cooking, and on a tight deadline—we were about to tape a new intro with me wearing the same clothes as the shoot, and drop it in. But Randy dropped a bomb in my lap.

I had questions about the fax that Randy had shown me, the July 2001 letters to Senator Graham's office, and Representative Wexler.

I asked Glass why he told Senator Graham that he was

gravely concerned: "I've told you repeatedly about my terrorist case—the sophisticated weapons system-nuclear components—the threats of blowing up the World Trade Center and who knows what else. These people hate Americans. This information I've gotten from the State Department about the airplanes being used...."

Wait a minute.

We were talking about Pakistani spy-terrorists. Since when are we talking about the "State Department" having "information" about "planes being used"?

That Friday, Glass told me:

"The only information that the terrorists—the guys ever talked about—was just the World Trade Center. They didn't ever say anything to me or to Dick, to my knowledge, that airplanes were going to be used. The State Department guy told *me* that. In other words, I called up and I bluffed him. I called up and I don't know *what* they knew that I knew. I just knew that America was going to be attacked. I didn't know if it was going to be the World Trade Center or what it was going to be. These people had talked about purchasing these weapons to use against us."

Based on what I knew of Iran/Contra and the BCCI, I threw Glass a curveball to see what he'd say. "When Dick Stoltz on 'Dateline' says stuff like, 'Well gee, we really thought that FBI or CIA would take over this case,' is it possible that the reason that the CIA didn't take over this case is because the CIA has been working with Pakistani intelligence?"

Glass replied, "Of course. That was the whole thing...the State Department was the vehicle that was used to shut down the case."

According to Glass, the criminal complaint written by the FBI's Steve Burdelski and the ATF's Steve Barborini against Mohsen, Malik, and Ingram was written in full detail. Bosses at FBI and higher-ups at the State Department ordered the complaint "sanitized" of all references to Pakistan. Instead of implicating the agents of the ISI, all uses of the word "Pakistan" were changed to "a foreign country." The complaint suffers from vagueness as a result. According to Glass, Agent Barborini was upset that his thirty-month-long sting operation had to conclude in a toothless criminal complaint.

Glass continued, "You'll see there's no mention of Pakistan. There's no mention of us showing them plutonium. There's no mention that incriminates Pakistan. I mean, Pakistan is not in there one time. And these were all Pakistani people who were here."

What happened next in my interview with Glass deserves to

be printed verbatim:

GLASS: When I called the State Department, I said to them, "Listen, I already know about the World Trade Center." So they assumed that I knew more than I did. And I didn't. I didn't know anything about airplanes.

HICKS: Who were you talking to at the State Department?

GLASS: This guy Chuck Hunter, and then this other guy. And to be honest with you, I couldn't tell you his name.

HICKS: Because you don't want to tell me his name? You don't think it would be prudent?

GLASS: Well, there's two reasons. I know who it is, but he didn't want to tell me. But I had my ways, and I found out.

HICKS: OK.

GLASS: So the bottom line is that if you check—and I've told so many people this, all you have to do is pull my phone records, I'll sign any release—there were at least six phone calls. And we're not talking thirty-second "Hi—how are you—I can't talk about it—goodbyes," we're talking lengthy phone calls. At least half a dozen.

HICKS: So you bluffed and you kind of pretended you knew more than you did. And then what did they tell you?

GLASS: But I didn't even have to do that. I just said what I knew. I said, "Look. Listen, I know the World Trade Center is going to be attacked." And then this guy said to me, "*Randy, listen, you cannot mention any of these things, especially airplanes being used to fly into the World Trade Center.*" And when he said that I almost fell off of my fucking chair. I mean, you have no idea. I thought I was gonna wear the tape out.

Later, Glass said his State Department contact explained that:

"[Pakistani President] Musharraf just took over and our position is that they're a nuclear power and they've been flexing their nuclear muscles with India and we are trying to prevent a nuclear catastrophe. And we know about the threat, the terrorist threat, from Al Qaeda and bin Laden flying air planes into the World Trade Center. And Musharraf has guaranteed us—because it's his ISI behind it—that he can stop it if we support him publicly.

"Look Randy, we know you're a straight guy, so we're going to give you some information. You cannot do two things: You cannot go to the media under any circumstance. This is—we're playing in a nuclear minefield now. Secondly, you can't tell the agents that you're working with now because they're cut out of the loop. They know nothing."

A KISS GOODBYE FROM THE FBI

After the Feds blew his cover, and Mohsen and Malik were slapped on the wrist, Glass went to jail for seven months, a reduced sentence for having served as a federal informant. Glass's millionaire heiress wife divorced him.

Right before Christmas '04, Glass was having trouble sleeping in a new place. "My parents are dead and my kids are dysfuntional and grown," he told me. Plus, his current girlfriend had gotten a restraining order against him, in order to avoid being evicted from his house.

I kept in touch with Glass all throughout the fall. I taped all of our conversations, and wound up with quite a box of cassettes.

Every time I asked myself why Glass was talking this much to me, I remembered the streams of vitriol he had poured out to me time and again, how the FBI used and discarded him. They exposed his undercover status to the likes of "Manson-types" like Diaa Mohsen. After thirty months behind bars, today Mohsen is out. Glass has it from a good source that Mohsen is "still active" and is "operating again." When I asked him if he felt threatened by the criminals he helped imprison, Glass said, "To be honest, I'm more worried about the government."

In light of his undercover service to the Bureau, it's curious that Glass hasn't been put into the Witness Protection Program. According to sealed court records, Glass's FBI handlers confirmed that Mohsen threatened Randy: he would be killed, "you know, if wrong things happened."

In February 2005, Glass related to me a telling anecdote. Glass had called Junior Ortiz, Bureau Chief of the Miami FBI office, complaining that he hadn't been informed of a few recent arrests of people who will threaten Glass's safety when they get out. When Junior Ortiz called back, Glass got it on tape as Ortiz barked: "We don't work for you. We don't have to tell you shit. We don't have to tell you about our investigation. We don't have to tell you who we arrest...don't ever fuckin' call this office again."

Glass responded, "Hey, just a minute! You fuckin' asshole! You don't work for me? I'm an American citizen, you fucking asshole! You work for the FBI, which is a government agency, and I'm an American citizen! You work for the American people! Who do you think you work for? The secret police? This isn't Nazi Germany."

"Don't ever fuckin' call this office again!" Ortiz retorted, and then hung up.

I asked Glass if he felt the FBI wanted him to get hurt. "Strong possibility," he answered.

THE PUPPET MASTER

Throughout December 2004, Glass was reticient to talk too specifically about the State Department higher-up who knew about "planes being flown into the World Trade Center." But each time we spoke, Glass revealed a little more.

In time, I learned the contact was one of Colin Powell's right-hand men. Glass said that the guy was African-American, and that his vocal manner on the phone had been prim and professional. Glass described him as Powell's own former "head of security," which at first was a mysterious term.

Given those criteria, and some Internet research, it became pretty clear that the identity of Glass's State Department source was most likely Francis X. "Frank" Taylor, currently the Assistant Secretary for Diplomatic Security at the State Department, as well as Director of the Office of Foreign Missions. On July 13, 2001, Taylor officially started at State Department, as Coordinator for Counterterrorism.

In May 2002, Frank Taylor went on a major diplomatic trip to Pakistan with then-National Security Advisor Condoleezza Rice, Attorney General John Ashcroft, and Assistant Secretary of State for South Asia Christina Rocca. The official purpose of the trip was to form a joint task force against terrorism. According to his official bio: "Prior to his appointment to the Department of State, Ambassador Taylor headed the Air Force Office of Special Investigations, where he was responsible for providing all Air Force commanders independent professional investigative services in fraud, counterintelligence, and major criminal matters." The Joint Inquiry on 9/11 thought enough of Taylor to have him testify in October 2002.

With his background as a top Air Force intelligence official, and his fast ascendance working as a high-powered diplomat to Pakistan, it seems that Taylor was running with the major players even before his official appointment on July 13, 2001. He may well have spoken with Glass right before Glass hand-wrote his July 2 fax memo.

On December 31, 2004, I asked Randy Glass point blank if his contact at State Department had been Frank Taylor.

Glass wasn't comfortable naming names, "Um...it might be, and you know, it might be better just to let it lie. Let's put it this way, all right. I am not actively doing stuff, OK, right now. I also don't want to burn—let's put it this way—there are guys in the intelligence community who I would never tell stories about or tell their names or tell you a story that would lead back to what could have only come from their department or them."

Later in the interview, I proposed we do this: "I can put it in the book in a way that I did the research and all evidence is pointing towards this person who Randy talked about—and didn't name-but all evidence points to this being Frank Taylor. Maybe that's the way it'll have to be in the book."

Randy answered promptly, "That's entirely fine."

THE STONE THE BUILDERS REJECTED

One of the principles that the FBI, CIA, et. al. follow is that, if the informant has a criminal past, no one in the mainstream media will take that person seriously as a whistle-blower. In most cases, this works; according to the logic of bourgeois propriety, it's not proper to believe someone if they have been convicted of a crime. It's an unforgiving, cold logic. It's an attitude that runs counter to the timeless wisdom of Psalm 118, the one Jesus of Nazareth quoted, in his axiom, "The stone the builders rejected has become the cornerstone."

U.S. intelligence uses certain procedures to execute operations and cover its tracks. Throughout this book, I will attempt to sketch out a few consistent patterns to the way in which former intelligence operatives and informants are treated after being used by the U.S. intelligence establishment. Despite his con man past, his rough edges, and his thick Baltimore accent, Glass was affectionately named the "Jewish Joe Pesci" by *Talk* magazine. As we'll learn in Chapter 11, Glass testified before a secret session of the House/Senate Joint Inquiry on 9/11, in a sealed room, off the record.

For all the pressure on low-level agents like ATF Steve Barborini to follow orders and turn on Randy Glass, Barborini was relatively supportive of Glass when I called him up, back in June 2004. The conversation quickly turned to the FBI's David Frasca, whose name kept coming up among 9/11 with FBI whistle-blowers. But before he worked out of Washington's FBI headquarters, Frasca was the head of the "Terrorism Task Force" in Miami. Barborini remembered him very well, and declined to comment, but he did so in a pretty telling way:

> **BARBORINI:** I can't. I can't. I'm not allowed to give a comment. He works for another agency, besides.
>
> **HICKS:** I know who he works for.

The Big Wedding:

BARBORINI: Not allowed to. Whether I feel good or bad about him I can't. He'd burn me.

HICKS: What can you tell me about Randy Glass?

BARBORINI: He does a lot of good things but I think he embellishes a little on certain things. You may want to call Richard Greenberg at "Dateline." He can do a lot more than I can. He's privy to a lot of documents that certain government agencies...we gave them to Greenberg, through certain ways, so we could confirm some of this stuff. He'll call you back, he's a good guy...I'm not allowed to....

HICKS: I totally understand, you're still working...

BARBORINI: I'm still working for ATF...

HICKS: I guess the issue becomes—at what point do American patriots, people who really care about this country, at what point do we stand up and say Dave Frasca is continually being accused by FBI whistle-blowers of deliberately foiling these investigations into Al-Qaeda-linked and ISI-linked....

BARBORINI: Yeah I don't know where he is right now is he still in headquarters? Probably buried somewhere.

HICKS: No, Frasca got promoted after 9/11!

BARBORINI: No way.

HICKS: Yeah!

BARBORINI: Really.

HICKS: He's number three in charge of domestic terrorism!

BARBORINI: That's why I like to fight to stay on the bottom; at least we can do good work.

HICKS: Oh my Lord....

BARBORINI: Exactly. Better off, believe me.

HICKS: Well, [Robert] Mueller, according to the Kerry Commission's report in '92, was head of the Criminal Division that deliberately foiled the Congressional investigation into BCCI. Then Mueller got promoted to head of FBI, so it's no surprise really that Frasca got promoted after 9/11, after being consistently accused of this kind of stuff. So, my question for you is: I can understand wanting to stay on the bottom and remain a part of almost a "blue collar" division of ATF. But the problem is, that means the fat cats and the more corrupt elements are the ones that are getting promoted and have the power.

BARBORINI: Well I'm sure at the organization you work for some of the people who can't do the work just get promoted. Call Richard Greenberg. I think he'd enlighten you on some things.[8]

8   Richard Greenberg repeatedly stated to me that he would do an on-the-record interview once he got clearance from NBC higher-ups. But when I tried to take him up on the offer, he stopped calling me back.

GLASS STILL ALIVE IN FLORIDA

Randy Glass indicated that he would be willing to play me what I started referring to as the "Frank Taylor Tapes," if I came down to Florida, after March 15, 2005. That's when Glass finished his probation. I started planning the trip down from New York.

Mike Ruppert, leading independent researcher of nefarious, narcotics-related U.S. intel operations, once wrote, "Out of maybe thirty men I have met over the years that have been connected with covert operations, only two have been total straight talkers."

Ruppert was explaining the complexities of con-man/spy Delmart Vreeland (whom we'll meet in Chapter 5).

Unlike Vreeland, Glass never mixed his con-man skills with his intelligence reporting to me. He never once lied, in the ten months I've spent researching him. He's slick, he's hella street smart, but he's got a heart of gold. A former con man, now he's a former spy, trying to live quietly in Florida. He's a stone the builders rejected. And his story about protected Pakistani spies is a big window into understanding 9/11.

CHAPTER 2

THE RIDDLE OF PAKISTAN:
BCCI, ISI, CIA

As the Bank of Credit and Commerce International (BCCI) fell apart in the early '90s, it left a trail of bodies in its wake. New York DA Robert Morgenthau counted a total of sixteen reporters and investigators who died while seeking the truth about it.[9]

BCCI was more than a bank. Like Enron, BCCI is an example of the form that mega-capital takes in contemporary times. BCCI was the funding vehicle the American and Pakistani intelligence used during the Soviet/Mujahedeen Afghanistan civil war. Ever since, this "client" relationship between CIA and Pakistan's ISI is the biggest scandal you've never heard of.

No wonder the U.S. media won't examine this simple fact: the day before the 9/11 attacks, the head of Pakistan's ISI, General Mahmood Ahmad, through his middleman, Saeed Sheikh, wired $100 thousand to Mohamed Atta, according to *Times of India* and Agence France-Presse. Both reported the incident on October 9, 2001. Later reports had the money funneled from ISI to the 9/11 hijackers closer to $325 thousand. Under U.S. pressure, General Ahmad was forced to resign shortly after the revelations.

Major General Vinood Saighal, who retired recently from the Indian Army, refers, in his multiple books on terrorism, to the ISI, Taliban, and Al Qaeda as one big "combine."[i] The ISI scandal is a major insight into understanding this "combine." After all, it killed 2,986 people on 9/11. So why haven't we heard of this wire transfer in "acceptable" media channels? Perhaps because it's so hot: almost everyone in the media/ intelligence/government elite knows the ISI can't be isolated from its relationship to the CIA. Mainstream media commentators often call the ISI a "state within a state" in Pakistan. A more accurate, and unpopular analysis would point out that the ISI is still a client state of the CIA. Senator Bob Graham, who acknowledged on live television that Randy Glass had warned

9   Jonathan Beaty and S.C. Gwynne, *The Outlaw Bank: A Wild Ride into the Secret Heart of BCCI* (New York: Random House, 1993)

his office about "planes being flown into the World Trade Center,"[ii] found himself in a meeting with this same ISI Chief General Mahmood Ahmad (and future CIA Director Porter Goss) on the morning of 9/11, as the attacks were under way.

The one time these anomalies crept up near mainstream news, the White House actively censored General Ahmad's name from the official transcript. "ISI Chief" Ahmad was mentioned at a White House press conference on May 16, 2002, when an Indian reporter asked National Security Advisor Condoleezza Rice about General Ahmad's September 10 wire transfer: "Are you aware of the reports at the time that the ISI chief was in Washington on September 11, and on September 10, $100 thousand was wired from Pakistan to these groups here in this area? And why was he here? Was he meeting with you or anybody in the Administration?"[10]

Condi Rice breezed by the sticky part of the question regarding the wire transfer. "I have not seen that report, and he was certainly not meeting with me," she answered. Thanks.

Yet instead of printing that exchange for the record, the White House's version of the transcript reads: "Are you aware of the reports at the time that (inaudible) was in Washington on September 11th, and on September 10, $100 thousand was wired from Pakistan to these groups here in this area?"[iii] That reference to "the ISI Chief" is the only "inaudible" thing in the whole transcript!

Pakistan, a nuclear power, is nominally a U.S. ally, thanks to its use as a staging ground when the USA helped create the "Soviet Vietnam" of the Afghan Civil War. For about nine years, the CIA worked with the ISI to funnel Saudi money to Afghan warlords and Islamic fundamentalists. Islamic nations like Egypt and Saudi Arabia emptied their prisons so that undesirables might go to Afghanistan to die as martyrs. Ronald Reagan called them "freedom fighters," but anyone living in the real world saw that the social-democratic government of Barbak Kamal had brought literacy, social services, and suffrage for women. The Mujahedeen changed all that once they took power. The U.S. promptly withdrew following the 1988 Soviet withdrawal. The feudal warlords fought amongst themselves for about seven years until 1992, when the Afghan government fell and the country devolved into chaos and brutal clan warfare. A grassroots movement of village and country-dwelling Muslims organized to take over the country. They were called the Taliban, which can be translated "people of the Book" or "religious students." The ISI convinced the CIA to back them. By 1996 the

10 Federal News Service, May 16th, 2002.

The Big Wedding:

Taliban had control of the whole country.

Back when the Taliban were still in embryonic form as the Mujahedeen, the "freedom fighters" took advantage of the giant river of heroin trafficking in the region, and just like the CIA did during Vietnam, milked heroin as a cash cow. When the *New York Times* reported the Mujahedeen were presiding over increased amounts of opium crops, the Mujahedeen came to Washington, complained about the *Times* at a press conference, and met with Vice President Bush.[11] According to a French military leader's memoirs,[12] William Casey and President Reagan approved a plan to get Soviet soldiers in Afghanistan addicted to the heroin confiscated by federal agents.

Once in power, the Taliban never did cut back on heroin production, despite a public image of fundamentalist asceticism. In October 2001, the Bureau of International Narcotics and Enforcement Affairs counted $40 million made by the Taliban by taxing opium farmers in 1999 alone. UN satellite photos showed that opium cultivation grew by 50 percent in 2000, according to *Reaping the Whirlwind,*[iv] a well-received book by Michael Griffin, a former Afghanistan-based consultant for UNICEF.

Likewise, the ISI still traffics in smack—the UN estimated that they pull down a cool $2.5 billion a year from the sale of illegal drugs.[13] In BCCI's heyday, the "Black Network" helped run guns into Pakistan that were paid for in heroin shipped back out. When Randy Glass first began dealing with R.G. Abbas and other ISI agents, they asked Glass if he would be willing to accept payment for guns and bombs in heroin.

In *Against All Enemies*, former White House terrorism expert Richard Clarke criticizes the U.S.'s perfunctory departure from Afghanistan. It was pragmatic and sudden and it helped create 9/11. Clarke writes that the CIA today is too dependent on the ISI; one could even say that the ISI is the eyes and ears of the CIA in the region. According to leading academics, the ISI cannot appoint its director without CIA approval.[14] Clarke criticizes the CIA for importing Arab extremists whom it did not understand into the Afghan Mujahedeen. Then, writes Clarke, when the Soviet Union retreated, and then imploded, the U.S. pulled out and was gone. Afghanistan was left without water, food, medicine, or security. Next door, Pakistan could have used some help stabilizing itself while it coped with millions of Afghan refugees, mixing with thousands of radicalized Arab Muslims.

After 9/11, President Musharraf and the ISI helped with the invasion of Afghanistan, after a big payoff in the form of U.S.

11 Bernard Gwertzman, "Afghans Put Case Before Forum," the *New York Times,* June 19, 1986
12 Counte de Marenches and David A. Andelman, *The Fourth World War: Diplomacy and Espionage in the Age of Terrorism* (New York: William Morrow & Co.)
13 *Times of India,* November 29, 1999
14 from Ruppert's *Rubicon:* "I was not surprised when [Professor] Michel Chossudovsky told me in a 2001 conversation that by verbal agreement each new head of the ISI had to receive the personal blessing of the director of Central Intelligence."

aid. Musharraf warned the U.S. that supporting the new war against the Taliban would cost him dearly at home, so the U.S. expressed its love the only way it knew how: it granted Pakistan a $3 billion aid package. Three billion to the same country who in June 1999 had an intelligence officer in New York City surrounded by FBI undercovers as he pointed at the World Trade Center and said "those towers are coming down." Three billion to the same country whose nuclear scientist, A.Q. Khan, developed nuclear technology and shared it with Iran, North Korea, and Lebanon. Three billion to the country who had wired one hundred thousand dollars to Mohammed Atta on September 10, 2001.

Three billion dollars can go a long way, but not everyone in Pakistan went along. In 2001, in the hotly contested territory of Kashmir, the ISI still had jihadists and Islamic extremists intent on liberating Kashmir from India, by any means necessary. And the ISI today is still full of pro-Palestinian militants enraged at Israel's expansionist policies. So, $3 billion meant nothing to the politics of the anti-Western, anti-crusaders of the ISI who had fought in Afghanistan against the Soviets and returned there in 2001 to help the Taliban resist the U.S. invasion. At the end of the conflict, in November 2001, Pakistan found that members of its ISI were trapped behind Afghanistan's rapidly crumbling enemy lines. They begged the U.S. to approve an airlift of about 3,300 Pakistani spies and officers out of Kunduz. The U.S. obliged, in a move that further proves the strength of the CIA/ISI relationship. The U.S. secured a corridor for the flights. Several Al Qaeda fighters and Taliban government officials also hitched a ride out of the country on these airlifts.

The *New Yorker* article by Seymour Hersh that first broke this story includes excuse-making from the U.S. regarding Taliban hitching along with ISI: "According to a senior intelligence official, 'Dirt got through the screen.'"[15] Which prompts one to ask, what screen? The CIA and ISI have been having sex without a condom since 1979. There is no screen. There has never been any screen.

Perhaps this is the perfect image of the CIA/Pakistan/Al Qaeda/Taliban combine: 3,300 of the U.S.'s alleged enemies flying over their attackers, the U.S. Army grunts, in aircraft flying at U.S. taxpayer expense. General Ahmad not only knew of the 9/11 attacks in advance, he funded them. The CIA and ISI have a tight, working relationship, bonded in the blood of battle against the Soviets. The question no one is asking here is what

15 Seymour Hersh, "The Getaway: Questions surround a secret Pakistani airlift," January 28, 2002, *The New Yorker*, www.newyorker.com/fact/content /?020128fa_FACT

The Big Wedding:

did Ahmad's contacts inside CIA knew about the 9/11 attacks?

It seems more and more likely that, when Frank Taylor[16] told Randy Glass that "we know all about planes being flown into the World Trade Center,"[17] among his sources were the State Department and the State Department's in-house liaison to the ISI, the CIA.

Unbelievably, even after the airlift, the ISI is still allowed to support the Taliban. In early May 2004, the *Times of London* reported that the Taliban-in-exile had launched a publicity campaign. After the "War in Iraq" had knocked them from international prime time, the Taliban were hungry for media. They suspended their edicts against television and issued camcorders to the pro-Taliban reporters embedded with their Taliban resistance fighters. *Times* Reporter Christina Lamb, who had once been ejected from Pakistan for getting too close to the ISI, wrote that the Taliban got their new digital cameras from Pakistan's ISI.[17]

Later, on May 10, 2004, the *Times of London* reported that they had discovered a twentieth hijacker who was supposed to participate in the 9/11 attacks. This one, Niaz Khan, was different: he had connections to the ISI, Kashmir, and mosques in Oldham, UK. In Lahore, Pakistan, he had been trained how to take over passenger airplanes.

At $3 billion over five years, the U.S. aid package makes Pakistan the third-biggest recipient of U.S. foreign aid, second only to Israel and Egypt. "If you just write a blank check it will end up in the pockets of the wrong people," said Representative Jim McDermott, as he watched the check being written, in 2001. Mr. McDermott doesn't seem to understand that this check for $3 billion was part of a much bigger pattern.[18]

HOW DID WE GET HERE?

When Ronald Reagan came to Washington as President-elect, he stirred things up by appointing his seventy-eight-year-old campaign director William Casey as head of the CIA. Casey became known for unapproved "off the shelf" operations (like the use of heroin as a weapon). These projects used back channels, black methods, and clandestine funding sources.

Around the same time, out of Pakistan, a new bank was gaining speed as an empowering, third world capital source. The Bank of Credit and Commerce International (BCCI) was origi-

---

16 "Frank Taylor" is the name we'll use from here on in to refer to the State Department source that Randy indicated was Francis "Frank" Taylor, but was not at liberty to confirm 100 percent on the record.

17 Christina Lamb and Mohammed Shehzad Islamabad, "Taliban Use the Devil's Weapons," May 2, 2004

18 He has since been retired due to re-districting.

nally chartered to be the first major bank dedicated to uplifting the poorer nations of Asia and Africa. But, in time, BCCI became much more than just a "bank" in the traditional sense. Similar to the ISI, with which it worked hand in glove, BCCI became more like a "state within a state." But then again, it was uncontainable by national borders. It was the perfect expression of capital in the age of empire: its powers usurped and made irrelevant the regulatory functions of the outdated nation-state.

In fact, BCCI grew at such a mutant pace that it started to ape the CIA. *Outlaw Bank* authors S.C. Gwynne and Jonathan Beaty called it:

> "A vast, stateless, multinational corporation that deploys its own intelligence agency, complete with a paramilitary wing and enforcement units, known collectively as the Black Network. It maintains its own diplomatic relations with foreign countries through bank 'protocol officers' who use seemingly limitless amounts of cash to pursue Abedi's goals."

"Abedi" would be Hasan Agha Abedi, the Pakistani founder. Abedi cultivated a mystique about himself that contributed to his power. As a Sufi, the branch of Islam that emphasizes love, humanism, and mystical powers, Abedi was rumored to be able to hypnotize audiences so thoroughly they would hallucinate. Supposedly, he could open doors without touching them. After a few beers, detectives for Robert Morgenthau's office told an *Outlaw Bank* author they suspected that Abedi was the antichrist.[20]

A case could be made for this, not because Abedi had spiritual powers, but because Abedi's story is the classic "Faustian bargain." Abedi might not be the Antichrist, but he certainly sold his soul. He traded his original vision of a Third World empowerment vehicle for a secretive, powerful, clandestine web where international arms dealers, CIA officers, narcotics traffickers, and Reagan/Bush operatives gathered like spiders. Abedi sacrificed his gifts of intelligence and social connections for mega-wealth, power, and influence. He created a cult-like company culture similar to Enron's, which collapsed almost exactly ten years later. What originally started out as a theocratic corporate structure that sought to put God first in all dealings soon degenerated into a company that acquired girls as young as twelve as favors for its clients.[21]

Like Enron or the CIA, BCCI was a multi-layered network of front companies (In this way, it was similar to certain Florida aviation companies we encounter later.) By the time the Bank of England wanted to shut it down, in the early '90s, BCCI had

19 Jonathan Beaty and S.C. Gwynne, *The Outlaw Bank: A Wild Ride into the Secret Heart of BCCI* (New York: Random House, 1993), 271.
20 ibid. (p. 267)
21 ibid.

The Big Wedding:

gained majority ownership of First American Bank. BCCI was a secretive multi-billion-dollar scam. It was the logical conclusion of the dog-eat-dog capitalism it sprang from. When BCCI's ownership of First America first came to light, regulators at the FDIC feared that busting BCCI it would create a run on the entire domestic U.S. banking industry. If $20 billion isn't where it claims to be, and the public finds out, it would be a FDIC regulator's worst nightmare. They feared the entire FDIC insurance fund would get sucked over the falls. In 1991, the regulators suddenly realized that the system was as vulnerable as it had been in 1929.

A Pakistani source told the award-winning authors of *Outlaw Bank* that BCCI and the ISI should be understood to be "practically the same" organization. A relationship with BCCI was at times more useful than a relationship with the CIA. Through its contacts at BCCI, the ISI gained the ability to hack into and download data from U.S. surveillance satellites.[22]

Beaty and Gwynne got a government source to tell them, "Several people in the State Department have resigned over the years in protest to the extent of our tilt to Pakistan. We gave them unauthorized satellite and communications technology as well as authorized sophisticated technology like the F-16 fighter plane sale. We ignored the drug trading and their nuclear bomb program, and your friend Abedi and BCCI were in the middle of all of it."[23]

Gwynne and Beaty got a big break from a source they named Ali Khan. Khan spoke on condition of anonymity; he didn't want to end up the latest victim to BCCI. During a breakthrough moment with the *Outlaw Bank* authors, Khan describes the bank's "Black Network":

> "You would have to understand how it was in Pakistan, and in Karachi, during the Afghanistan war. BCCI was working with your CIA. Abedi and the bank are interwoven with Pakistan's intelligence agency, and Inter-Services Intelligence was in charge of supplying the Afghan fighters. Abedi was dealing directly with William Casey. I know he met with Casey in Washington, several times, I think they were all great friends. Pakistan received a great amount of military technology from the United States that was under the table."[24]

But BCCI shouldn't be blamed entirely on the Republicans. Its senior representative in the U.S., Clark Clifford, was a Democratic powerbroker, attorney, and informal advisor to almost every President since Truman. In 1947, he helped draft the National Security Act, which created the CIA. He advised

22 ibid. (p.238)
23 ibid. (p. 255)
24 ibid. (p. 262)

President Johnson in 1967 regarding the Six-Day War in the Middle East, when Israel took on Egypt, Jordan and Syria in 1967.[25] BCCI was a manifestation of global capital. BCCI was the product of a class in decline, not one party. Although its ostentatious behavior and corruption are mimicked in the corporate scandals of today, but BCCI set records that have yet to be surpassed. BCCI took in Democrats and Republicans alike, as plutocrat moths to the flame.

Clifford cashed out of BCCI in 1988, after Iran/Contra had broken in the media. He made $21.6 million and eventually received a slap on the wrist when the ceiling fell in '91. Democrat Bert Lance was highly involved, as he pimped domestic banks to BCCI. Lance was an old friend of President Jimmy Carter and worked for BCCI during Carter's term.

Senator John Kerry investigated BCCI as part of his work on the Senate Foreign Relations Committee, but Kerry only went so far. He pointed out that the Criminal Division of the Department of Justice (headed by Robert Mueller) had fought him every step of the way in stymieing his access to documents. But then again, Kerry himself took a $5 thousand donation from Clark Clifford and partner Robert Altman the same month that he defanged his own investigation by letting his key investigator go. That investigator, the fatalistic Jack Blum, had the motto on his wall, "Never wrestle a pig, you get dirty and the pig likes it."[26]

Just as Bert Lance was BCCI's right hand man in the Carter White House, Jackson Stephens was right hand man to Bill Clinton. Stephens also did a big favor for young George W. Bush when Bush needed to unload $25 million of Harken Energy stock. Stephens sold the Harken stock to BCCI banks and a Saudi connection, Sheikh Abdullah Bakhsh. (Stephens' name also came up when I traveled to Venice, Florida to visit the strange little town where Mohamed Atta went to flight school. There, I learned of the long history the Venice Municipal Airport has with U.S. intelligence covert operations and narcotics trafficking. For some reason, the former headquarters of Jackson Stephens's Beverly Enterprises was located next door.)

Jackson Stephens' getting Saudi money to young Dubya Bush while at Harken was somehow fitting. This Sheikh Bakhsh had been a banker to Sheikh Khalid bin Mahfouz. Bin Mahfouz had originally funded Dubya's first oil venture back in 1978, when he sent $50 thousand through his American representative James Bath. Sheikh Khalid bin Mahfouz later became the majority shareholder of BCCI.

BCCI was so big that it even burned the U.S. State

25 ibid. (p.154-6)
26 ibid.

Department and CIA. When it burst into flames, it took down $10 million of U.S. Agency for International Development funds.[27] The Kerry Committee suggested that Jackson Stephens was "BCCI's Principal U.S. Broker," since he, his company, and his henchmen, guided BCCI's first acquisitions of U.S. banks.

Speaking of bin Mahfouz, BCCI, and Bush, let's return to a topic I touched on in my Introduction: Bill White, the former business partner of James Bath. Recall that Bath was the intermediary between BCCI's Sheik bin Mahfouz and Salem bin Laden.

Bill White blew open the Bush/bin Laden connection on the Canadian Broadcasting Corporation's "The Fifth Estate," in an interview with Bob McKeown in October, 2003. Despite having been bankrupted in rigged Texas courts, White was still willing to talk about his firsthand experiences with Bath/Bush/bin Laden. Hatfield had it right, and there's much more. Young Dubya didn't just take a measly $50 thousand dollars from Bath on behalf of Salem bin Laden and Sheik Khalid bin Mahfouz. James Bath was in fact controlling "six to seven million dollars" of Saudi money belonging to those Saudi investors.

Now that young Bush was president, White was ready to claim:

> "the money that changed hands back during my experiences with Bath...influenced or clouded or even compromised the president's ability to wage war against terrorism. I just can't imagine how he can be an objective arbitrator of the bin Laden family's activities when in fact he's taken money from them that's never been reported publicly. And I think he's compromised. And that's of great concern to me. And I think that's a great concern to the families of the victims of the 9/11 tragedy."

White first decided to break with Bath in 1992. White threatened to go public. Bath promised to destroy him.

According to White, Bath said,

> "Now I know you being Mom and apple pie think that America's about truth and justice but that's nothing but a bunch of horse ptooey. [He said] if we sue you, number one, you're not going to have money to pay the lawyers to defend yourself against these lawsuits, and number two, in the unlikely event that you could ever get legal representation, all it would take is a call from George Bush to these Republican judges who are beholden to him, his political appointees...you'll never get a chance to tell this story to a jury. You'll never even get a day in court."

---

27   ibid.

White didn't go public. Bath sued him anyway. In the end, White was bankrupted and drained.

> "It's cost me virtually everything, financially. I lost my business, all my real estate holdings, all of my assets were conveyed to Bath in the lawsuits, my house was foreclosed on because the mortgage was held by the bank that was laundering the Saudi money, all my property was sold at cost wholesale, and we paid a terrible price."

White was so close to the Bush/bin Laden connection that he could feel its dry, radiating heat in his face. At one point, Bath offered a sizable amount of hush money in exchange for White's silence and his signature on a settlement. Thinking of fallen comrades in Vietnam, White recalled their oath to defend the Constitution and said 'no.'[28]

In return for his valor, he was destroyed.

CIA/BCCI/ISI->MUJAHEDEEN/TALIBAN/AL QAEDA

Today, the CIA has denied having "any relationship whatsoever" with Osama bin Laden. It's a lie. And even MSNBC won't go along with that one anymore. To understand why a CIA/BCCI/ISI relationship exists today, let's look again at why it was created: the Mujahedeen. Which created the Taliban. Which helped to create Al Qaeda.

The Kerry Senate report on BCCI quotes a former Pakistani cabinet member who says, "It was Arab money that was pouring through BCCI." Like 9/11 itself, BCCI was a combination of Saudi money and Pakistani muscle.

According to a Nation article dated February 15, 1999, the U.S. and Saudi Arabia gave an estimated $40 billion to support the Mujahedeen guerrilla fighters opposing the Russians. "Most of the money [was] managed by the ISI, Pakistan's intelligence agency," Paul Thompson wrote online in the "9/11 Timeline."

Today, according to former CIA case officer Robert Baer, Saudi oil money has created a dysfunctional, plump society with 30 percent unemployment. Their corrupt, overpaid military has purchased massive amounts of hardware it never bothered to unpack, test, or train on.[29] The Pakistanis were just the opposite: one of the poorest countries on earth, a country born in the blood of the partition of India.

28 A corrected version of the CBC's transcript exists at
http://sanderhicks.com/billwhite.html
29 Robert Baer, *Sleeping with the Devil: How Washington Sold Our Soul for Saudi Crude* (New York: Crown, 2003)

The Big Wedding:

Before the Mujahedeen took over and created the Taliban, Afghanistan was not "Communist," per se. It was ruled by a social-democratic party called the People's Democratic Party (PDP). The PDP "declared a commitment to Islam within a secular state" and made great social improvements with literacy, equality of women, infant mortality, and land reform.

A counter-revolution against the PDP started breeding in the hills. Large landowners, royalists, and tribalists made false claims that the PDP had secret plans to curtail religious freedom. The *New York Times* stated that the religious issue was "being used by some Afghans who actually object more to President Taraki's plans for land reforms...." The United States began officially supporting Afghan fundamentalists, despite the fact they had kidnapped and killed the American ambassador, Adolph Dubs in February 1979.

The U.S. and Pakistan began training Mujahedeen at camps in Pakistan in 1978. One of the "holy warriors" the U.S. had on its side at this time was Osama bin Laden. Five years after arriving, he was running the Maktab al-Khadamat (MAK), which funneled international aid, cash, and CIA intelligence into the "anti-Communist" cause. MAK became the "primary conduit." According to Michael Moran, international editor at MSNBC, the MAK was nurtured and controlled by the ISI. So, not only did the CIA have a relationship with bin Laden, he was the CIA point man. The ISI was the CIA's "cutout," i.e., a middleman that could be blamed, if need be, if the heroin trading or illegal weapons brokering of BCCI ever broke in the mainstream press.

Meanwhile, in Kabul, the PDP's progressive President Taraki started begging Soviet Moscow for military aid, but Moscow didn't want an international incident. Six months later, Taraki was assassinated by a colleague, Hafizullah Amin, a PDP extremist. The Soviets claimed that Amin had CIA ties. The USSR entered the country on December 8, and killed Amin in his palace. They helped install Babrak Karmal, an original revolutionary from the 1978 uprising. On December 23, the *Washington Post* clarified "There was no charge [from the State Department] that the Soviets have invaded Afghanistan, since the troops apparently were invited."

So, a quick look at the *Washington Post* and the *New York Times* from the period shows us that "Soviet invasion" is not exactly a correct term. But in the wake of Vietnam, hawks in Congress wanted to get even. Representative Charlie Wilson led the pack with rationalizations like, "There were fifty-eight thousand dead in Vietnam...we owe the Russians one..." President Reagan started referring to the Mujahedeen as "freedom fighters" instead of feudal terrorists who shot down passenger airplanes. In 1986, the British hardliner Margaret Thatcher met formally with Abdul Haq, a Mujahedeen leader who had planted a bomb at Kabul airport in 1984, killing twenty-eight innocents. On September 24, 2001, Haq rejoined the Northern Alliance.

All of which recalls the hip-hop band Dead Prez's declamation:

"You wanna stop terrorists?
Start with the U.S. imperialists
Ain't no track record like America's, see
Bin Laden was trained by the CIA.
But I guess if you a terrorist for the U.S.
Then it's OK."

After all the carnage had rotted away and the smoke had cleared, certain U.S. power strategists had a chance to sit back and reflect what the civil war in Afghanistan had been all about. In his 1998 interview with *Le Nouvel Observateur,* Zbigniew Brzezinski, President Jimmy Carter's National Security Adviser, revealed that the CIA began destabilizing the pro-Soviet Afghan government six months earlier in a deliberate attempt to get the Soviets to invade. The Carter White House was in line with hawks in Congress: it was time for a Soviet Vietnam. Brzezinski asked, "What is most important to the history of the world? The Taliban or the collapse of the Soviet empire? Some stirred-up Muslims or the liberation of Central Europe and the end of the Cold War?"

9/11 answered that rhetorical question. 9/11 should have shattered that smug manipulative superiority forever.

The Big Wedding:

CHAPTER 3

DAN HOPSICKER VS. RUDI DEKKERS, WALLY HILLIARD, MOHAMED ATTA, AND THE FBI

Daniel Hopsicker is the kind of 9/11 researcher who stands head and shoulders above the rest of us tinkerers and speculators. The guy has laid his life on the line. After 9/11, he went to Florida, and started looking under some big rocks.

In his book and on his website, he asks questions that go straight to the heart of the issue around 9/11: how is it that three out of four terrorist pilots trained at flight schools owned by men with links to some of the most powerful people in the U.S.? Why is it that almost everyone who knew these terrorists-in-training has been visited by the FBI or the Florida Department of Law Enforcement, and told to change their story, shut up, or disappear for awhile?

Daniel Hopsicker used to produce TV for NBC. He's the author of *Barry and the Boys*, a rollicking rollercoaster ride of an investigation into Barry Seal, a little-known Iran/Contra figure who piloted multiple runs from U.S.-backed Contra airstrips in Honduras to CIA-protected drop zones in Arkansas, running a C-123 cargo plane full of cocaine. While researching *Barry and the Boys,* Hopsicker was warned that he was putting his life in danger. Sources were pressured not to talk. After all, Hopsicker was "threatening to compromise ongoing government operations." *Barry and the Boys* set the stage for Hopsicker to focus on the aviation crimes involved in 9/11. The result was *Welcome to Terrorland: Mohamed Atta and the 9/11 Cover-up in Florida.*

Raised in Chicago, young Hopsicker's folks moved him to the Bay area in his teens. He wanted to go to U.C. Berkeley and join the underground, but his dad said no way. Instead, Dan went to UCLA where he led the student strike during Nixon's bombing of Cambodia. Later, he explained to me, "I had seen protests in Berkeley led by people who knew how to do things. It was an invaluable education." Students turned over parked cars and took over the Administration building.

We first met when I announced the re-publication of *Fortunate Son* in 1999. Daniel Hopsicker was one of three independent researchers who came out of the woodwork to congratulate me. All three also imparted a sense of warning. Michael Ruppert (the LA anti-CIA narcotics trafficking researcher), James Sanders (the TWA Flight 800 expert), and Daniel Hopsicker were similar. They had been dealing in suppressed histories and had seen what this knowledge can do to people. All three had been laboring in isolation on some very big subjects. At that point, in '99 only Sanders had published a book. All three were iconoclastic, highly individualistic, scarred, bloodied, and unbowed.

Hopsicker's work is highly energetic, and driven. At their best moments, his books are page-turners of major "true crime." At their less than best moments, his books can be disorganized, repetitive, and written in a voice that is occasionally pretentious or jocular. Daniel loves using the "we" voice, that *New Yorker* voice of literary pseudo-authority. When pressed, Daniel insists he must be free to have his own style. One Internet critic calls that style "annoyingly breezy." (Of course, that same critic authored a comprehensive list: "Mohamed Atta Loved Pork Chops, and 49 Other Things You May Not Know About The 9/11 Florida Connection," based on Hopsicker's book; the list was posted on Democratic Underground[30]).

At lunch on the day that I met him, I sat back and tried to understand the frantic rant of this big, bald, blue-eyed guy. He reminded me of one of the old skinheads at punk shows in the bleak upper reaches of Northwest DC. At the end, he said the newspaper *The Spotlight* was selling his videos. I asked him why he was associated with a far-right newspaper. He said it

30 http://www.democraticunderground.com/discuss/duboard.php?az=view_all&address=1

The Big Wedding:

was just business, they were the only ones willing to sell his material. I said something my mom used to tell me, "You lay down with dogs, you end up smelling like dogs."

The same is true for "Masters of the Universe: The Secret Birth of the Federal Reserve," one of Hopsicker's five scruffy video documentaries. On the one hand, his work here is important and underreported: not enough of us have asked why a gaggle of international bankers, in a secret meeting in 1910, created a private bank to sell currency to the federal government. But in a less-than-thought-out move, Hopsicker chose to explore this topic with two far-right authors onscreen: Eustice Mullins and William Gill. In his book *The Curse of Canaan,* Mullins asserts that Jews and people of color were forever cursed by God, and states, in open advocacy of genocide, that it is "God's command" that white people should exterminate them. When asked why he chose these clowns to interview about the Federal Reserve, Hopsicker snapped that they were the leading critics of the Federal Reserve, and were the obvious choices.

In the summer of 2004, I hustled to get Hopsicker some serious media attention in New York for his research and new book on Atta. I was able to get him on the courageous "Majority Report" show on Air America radio and Court TV's "Crier Live." But the networks and the cable stations weren't biting, and the story never broke into mainstream consciousness. Daniel went back to Venice, back to living off his e-commerce in a bungalow with banana trees in the back. Hopsicker often complains "there is no media" in the USA.

Hopsicker had been visiting Venice, Florida since his parents bought a retirement home there in 1975. When he came back to Venice after 9/11, Hopsicker brought a mad bag of skills. His research into Barry Seal had given him a dry run for tracking aviation records. Barry Seal research was a crash course in CIA front-companies; especially the Florida proprietary cargo airlines involved in Iran/Contra, Bay of Pigs, CIA covert operations against Cuba, etc. The experience taught him how to track FAA flight plan records and airplane ownership. Unlike other 9/11 researchers who sat at computers and relied on others' Internet research, Hopsicker did something so rare, it can only be referred to with an archaic verb: he "gumshoed." That is, Hopsicker became a kind of independent detective quietly investigating the scene. Meanwhile, a certain part-time research consultant to an SEC task fed him corporate documents online.[31] Hopsicker gumshoed into government records offices, met with sources, and got the kind of documents and commentary you can

31 This SEC contact has also been a helpful source to myself as well. The contact requested anonymity due to the sensitivity of the investigation into international corporate corruption.

only pull down in person.

Hopsicker started with Rudi Dekkers. Dekkers is a Dutch citizen and an ex-con from a tax-evasion-related charge in his native Holland. He was the president of Huffman Aviation, which housed and trained two of the four 9/11 pilots. One of those pilots was 9/11 team leader Mohammed Atta. Dekkers was flamboyant and outspoken for the cameras right after 9/11, and when I talked to him, he claimed he had given over a thousand interviews, starting on 9/11.

Dekkers told the cameras that he only trained Atta for "like thirty or forty" hours, and then didn't see him for nine months. But in Venice, Daniel Hopsicker found a cab driver, Bob Simpson, who said he picked up Dekkers and Atta at the home of Iran/Contra pilot Charlie Voss. The cabbie dropped them all off together at Sharky's beachside bar, three weeks before 9/11.

Hopsicker unearthed court documents that demonstrate a noteworthy lack of character: Dekkers sexually harassed an eighteen-year-old employee of Huffman Aviation, Nicole Antini, and was found guilty in court. He then failed to pay the settlement, which made the harassment records public. Reading the greasy details of the harassment suit reveal that he's got the ethics of a snake. What kind of person would choose Rudi Dekkers to run a company? How is it that Rudi Dekkers was given "a thousand live interviews" on camera by a fawning corporate media?

In 2004, there were rumors going around that Rudi wanted a book deal, so I called him up. Dekkers came off as bluntly materialistic and insouciant: "My only reason to write a book is to make money." Over the course of our talk, Dekkers found me much too curious about 9/11. When I asked about Dekkers' former boss, Wally Hilliard, former owner of Huffman Aviation, Dekkers said,

"I know a lot about him of course. I don't think I have a lot on the table for what you're looking for into the political affairs and into a pissing contest with the government, no. I only want to put down the experience I have. I have experience from Ashcroft down to police in this matter, my experience. And my title could be something like 'How Could I Have Known?'"

Well, Rudi, let's see. John Ashcroft stopped flying commercial flights in June 2001. If you've got "experience" with Ashcroft, your title could be "How Could I Have NOT known?" In fact, according to a former office manager Hopsicker found, Rudi never came into work before 10 AM. Yet on the morning of

9/11 he was there unusually early with the TV on.

Before Dekkers hung up, he unwittingly revealed some new information about a visit to Venice by the twentieth hijacker, Zacharias Moussaoui.

> "The FBI investigated me about Moussaoui, and I called the FBI when I saw the picture on TV: 'that guy was in my facility.' They said 'It's impossible, he was outside the U.S. at that time.' I said, 'OK. I'm just telling you he was in my school'...Then six months later they came and asked me to testify in Washington that he was in my facility. I never heard anything anymore."

So you didn't testify about Moussoaui being there?

> "No."

Well, see, that's interesting, isn't it?

> "Yes, it is. But I'm just an airplane school owner, and I don't want to go in politics."

Well I'm afraid you already have. You don't choose politics. The political realities of the world choose you.

> "No, I know. But all I'm saying is that, if I write a book, I don't want to piss off anybody. I just want to say what my experience is."

With the publication of *Welcome to Terrorland,* Dekkers's financial mismanagement at Huffman and sexual harassment conviction reached book form. Hopsicker attended an arraignment and says Dekkers threatened him outside a Florida courthouse. The paunchy Dutchman waved his hands and whined, "I'm warning you, I'm warning you...you'll find out." Later, Dekkers threatened to sue Hopsicker for $25 million. He has yet to file suit.[32]

Dekkers, according to Hopsicker's research, was not exactly a ladies man. He also harassed Amanda Keller, the temporary girlfriend of Mohamed Atta. It took him a year, but Hopsicker tracked her down. Keller told Hopsicker that Atta was horrible in bed, had a small penis, wasn't all that interested in sex, and had something of a foot fetish. These sensational, trashy details made the front cover of the leading tabloid newspaper of the nation. But that nation was Germany. Here's a loose translation of how *Der Bild* tackled the topic:

> Wild months full of sex, drugs, alcohol, and violence started. Atta was wearing casual yuppie-clothes, was a casual drinker who beleaguered women in bars, spending money and buying drinks. For Atta, the spy who took flight lessons, sexy Amanda became more than just an accessory of his camouflage. Did the man, who already knew his date of death, fall in love? With Amanda, Atta made a three-day trip through the bars of Key West-without a second of sleep. He paid for everything, snorted cocaine with rolled dollar bills, and put money in strippers' G-strings. "He called me a pagan all the time," Amanda remembers.

32 For more on this, see sanderhicks.com for the interview transcript from Hopsicker and myself on INN World Report TV, on sanderhicks.com.

Right around this time, I sent *National Enquirer* Hopsicker's book, but they politely took a pass on covering the Atta and Amanda story. I wondered if that was a direct result of having their photo editor, Bob Stevens, murdered by the mysterious anthrax attacks.[33]

Like many other witnesses who knew Atta, Keller says she has been harassed by the Florida Department of Law Enforcement. Of course, Keller was never called as a witness by the 9/11 Commission. Everything she says about the man contradicts the official story. The FBI says that Atta left the area of Venice, Florida at the end of 2000, but just by digging through the local papers, Hopsicker points out that they lied: Atta lived with Amanda Keller in the Sandpiper Apartments, across the street from the Venice airport, in April 2001.

The FBI and the Florida Department of Law Enforcement have paid a visit to anyone who knew Atta and might challenge the official story. Atta's and Amanda's neighbor told Hopsicker, "At first, right after the attack, they told me I must have been mistaken, in my identification. Or they would insinuate that I was lying. Finally, they stopped trying to get me to change my story, and just stopped by once a week to make sure I hadn't talked to anyone." Amanda was eventually pressured into claiming that the Atta she knew and slept with was a different Mohamed Atta.

Through interviews with Keller, Hopsicker has drawn a painfully private picture of Atta, a man with some serious problems. His face says it all, deep, brooding anger under tons of

---

33 Although a full investigation into the 2001 Anthrax attacks is outside the scope of this book, the answers are out there—Peace activist and researcher John Judge pointed out the following about the attacks, "Anthrax didn't come from abroad, the trail led to the door of Fort Detrick and then it stopped. They realized from its DNA signature that it was 'Ames scree'—which means University of Iowa, which had an archive of all the known pathenogenic strains of Anthrax...It would have been possible to go back to Ames and figure out which particular batch this came from and then that batch would have had a paper trail of who had ordered that batch, but ten days before the first Anthrax

pressure. The official story from the FBI is that Atta was a fundamentalist Muslim who hated America and led the 9/11 attacks. In real life, however, Atta seemed to be something of an Egyptian double agent who fell in love with an American ex-stripper and did a lot of coke.

Hopsicker's Keller interviews, on video and in the book, report that Atta already had a full pilot's license when he came to Florida. He was a very Westernized playboy, going on three-day cocaine and booze binges in Key West with Amanda Keller. Bizarre behavior for a jihadist who allegedly wrote in his diary just before 9/11 that his corpse was not to be touched by female hands. The full implications of who and what the real Mohamed Atta was will be explored in Chapter 4. First, let's examine who owned Huffman Aviation, when Atta trained there.

MR. BIG

Just by the virtue of being there and reading the local newspapers, Hopsicker found that on July 25, 2000, the DEA in Orlando busted a crew with more than forty-three pounds of heroin inside a Learjet owned by Wally Hilliard, owner of Huffman Aviation. Earlier that month, on July 3, 2000, Atta and Marwan Al-Shehhi had started flight lessons with Rudi Dekkers at Huffman. Hopsicker claims that it's not a coincidence—Atta may have been involved in importing heroin with Hilliard's help, selling Afghanistan's notorious cash cow to finance Islamic terror.

"The FBI is protecting an operation set in place back in the '80s...a money-laundering device to funnel money to the Afghan Mujahedeen and to flood this country with heroin," Daniel told me in an interview. According to Hopsicker, the Venice operation was "protected" by top officials in the same U.S. government that created the Taliban, Hopsicker says that when low-level DEA agents burst into Hilliard's plane in Orlando on July 25, an embarrassed DEA higher-up (Mike Brassentine) was sitting in the co-pilot seat.

Federal agents stated in court that Hilliard's planes made at least thirty weekly trips to Venezuela before the bust in July. But Hilliard claimed innocence, saying the planes were leased to others. Neither Hilliard nor his business partner, Diego Levine-Taxar (the Learjet's pilot), did any time for the heroin. Instead, two "mules," i.e., low-level traffickers, were incarcerated. A

envelope was mailed, FBI contacted the University at Ames and convinced them to destroy the entire seventy-year archive. So, there's absolutely no paper trail left." A milder version of this was reported by a team at the *New York Times,* which included the language: "Shortly after the first case of Anthrax arose, the F.B.I. said it had no objection to the destruction of a collection of Anthrax samples at Iowa State University, but some scientists involved in the investigation now say that collection may have contained genetic clues valuable to the inquiry." [see William J. Broad, David Johnston, Judith Miller and Paul Zielbauer, "A Nation Challenged: The Inquiry, Experts See F.B.I. Missteps Hampering Anthrax Inquiry," *New York Times,* November 9, 2001]

Huffman Aviation-associated corporate shell, Brittania Aviation, "has a green light from the DEA," according to Hopsicker's aviation industry sources in Lynchburg, VA.

A web of larger corporate connections links Huffman owner, Wally Hilliard, to a world much bigger than small-town Venice, Florida. With a little help from the SEC consultant, I found that Hilliard did business with Myron DuBain. DuBain was chairman of the Fireman's Fund Insurance Company in 1981 when the company announced plans to acquire Employers Health, an insurance company co-founded by Hilliard, who was then chairman. Although the deal collapsed, the link to DuBain is noteworthy.

DuBain later became CEO of Amfac Parks and Resorts, (now Xanterra Parks and Resorts), which owned the Silverado Resort in the Napa, California wine country. The SEC consultant points out that Silverado often hosted Iran/Contra heavyweights Ollie North, Rob Owen (North's liaison to the Contras), and George H.W. Bush for golf and cocktails. "Silverado" was even the namesake of Neil Bush's disastrous savings and loan in Colorado.

My SEC contact worked at United California Bank (UCB) when Myron DuBain was on the board, right after former CIA director John McCone served as chairman. UCB had been on the brink of collapse, "under the weight of highly irregular loans." UCB had been known as John McCone's "piggy bank" and, with DuBain on board, they "attempted to recover monies looted and missing" by Saudi arms dealers (such as Adnan Khashoggi) and former CIA personnel.

According to Hopsicker's sources, right after 9/11, Huffman Aviation received a special visitor. Florida Governor Jeb Bush arrived, seized the terrorist pilots' records at Huffman Aviation School, ordered them onto a government cargo plane, and had them flown out of the country. I asked an eyewitness, Florida cop Tom McNulty, whether he would be willing to confirm Jeb Bush's presence on September 12, 2001 at Huffman. McNulty lowered his voice and said, "keep digging."

Wally Hilliard, the "Mr. Big" behind Huffman Aviation, had a strange propensity for business dealings with shady characters, like the Pakistani Pervez Khan, who had a clearance to fly to Havana and South America. Hilliard bought a $2 million plane from Clinton fund-raiser Truman Arnold for only one dollar.

When this was first discovered by Dan Hopsicker it didn't earn him any respect in mainstream media circles. But that's not a huge surprise. As soon as JFK was shot, the headlines read, "Young Leftist Apprehended." Over time, the official story about Oswald being a young Communist forcibly dissolved into Oswald being a very confused ex-marine, until eventually, leading scholars of the JFK hit came to believe Oswald was, like he claimed, "just a patsy."

Thanks to the work of Daniel Hopsicker, the cracks in the official story are beginning to show. At this moment in history, mainstream consciousness is still at the stage of "Atta was an Islamic fundamentalist." But as we meet more experts on military/intelligense operations in Florida (like in Chapter 11) it becomes apparent why Hopsicker named the state "Terrorland."

The Big Wedding:

CHAPTER 4

THE ENIGMA OF ATTA, AND THE PRECEDENT OF DOUBLE-AGENT EGYPTIANS

Mohamed Atta is remembered fondly by his classmate and friend, Mohamed Mokhtar El Rafei:

> He was a very helpful man, and friendly. So friendly...I have never found him annoying or something, or feeling that he don't want to share with people's pain. He was very helpful. He was a very good listening person. And he was completely polite. Polite with the complete meaning of this word, really. His raising up, as I knew, was surrounding with the most basics of morals. His father looked after him so much. He has only one sister, and his father is a very, very gentle and moral person.[34]

Amanda Keller reports a very different sort of person, a brooding psychopath who dismembered a litter of kittens in her apartment when she dumped him. What happened to Atta?

Atta is well-known in the U.S. media as the Islamic fundamentalist who wrote passionate and sectarian letters of protest when a female student was ejected from the American University at Cairo for wearing the niqab, or face-veil. How is it that this same fundamentalist broke Islamic law by shacking up with a Florida infidel he met at Papa John's Pizzeria?

The differences between Atta in the early '90s and Atta in 2000/2001 are striking. Which one is correct? And where did the false one come from? Why?

---

34 From the Australian Broadcasting Corporation interview with Liz Jackson archived at http://www.abc.net.au/4corners /atta/interviews/mukhtar.htm

The 9/11 Commission Report, with a sterilized tone, claims, "The FBI and CIA have uncovered no evidence that Atta held any fraudulent passports." It's almost as if the Commission is attempting to contradict what Amanda Keller told Daniel Hopsicker: Atta had passports from Egypt, the United Arab Emirates, and Saudi Arabia. Atta had a locked briefcase he kept with him at all times. Once, Keller saw inside it when Atta was nearby. She saw multiple pilots' licenses from various countries. One of the photos "didn't look anything like" Atta. Atta spoke English, Arabic, German, and French, and read Hebrew to her. This guy went to Hamburg, Germany, and spent seven years in "grad school" before submitting a dissertation.

Two pages earlier in *The 9/11 Commission Report*, it's asserted: "Atta and Shehhi both encountered some difficulty reentering the United States, on January 10 and January 18 [2001] respectively. Because neither presented a student visa, both of them had to persuade INS inspectors that they should be admitted so that they could continue their flight training. Neither operative had any problem clearing Customs."

Oh, really? The Commission would have us believe that Prince Charming himself, Mohamed Atta, had the ability to sweet-talk his way through Customs. Recall, we're talking about a guy who, on the morning of 9/11, "sent chills through" the spine of a ticket counter worker who hurriedly checked him into his flight. Later, that airline employee recalled, "You see his picture in the paper...you see more life in that picture than there is in flesh and blood."[35] That day in Miami, Atta somehow got customs to give him an eight-month extension of a visa that had already expired. Later, Atta helped a few of the other "muscle" hijackers get through Customs, by greeting their flight and walking them through. Nothing unusual here? Not if you read Israeli spy Ari Ben-Menache who wrote that the Miami airport was often set up with "pre-clearances" for intelligence assets, with flight-greeters sent to meet international operatives.[36]

The more I've looked into Atta, the more I realize that the truth about him is 180 degrees from what the big media and government spokespersons have presented. Before I expand upon the collection of facts about Atta, let's step back into the big picture for a minute.

Most people conceive of nation-states as discrete (meaning strictly-defined) entities, boxed in by their borders. But after studying international intelligence, it's clear that the nature of spying is to use multiple layers of case-officers, agents, assets, and informants. So, when the U.S. has an enemy like Al Qaeda,

35 David Hench, "Ticket Agent Haunted By Brush With 9/11 Hijackers," *Portland* (Maine) *Press Herald,* 6 March 2005
36 Ari Ben-Menashe, *Prophets of War: Inside the Secret U.S.-Israeli Arms Network* (New York: Sheridan Square Press, 1992)

The Big Wedding:

it will want to infiltrate and penetrate it with moles and spies who will send back reports.

And Al Qaeda, in turn, will be doing the exact same thing. Out of this duel, this duet, comes some bizarre characters who display the values and behaviors of both sides. The layers of duplicity create "double agents." You'd like to think that someone is keeping track of who is working for whom amid all the switching sides, backstabbing, and betrayal. Maybe the emerging principle of all this is that the most centralized, bureaucratized institutions end up producing the most chaos, while decentralized, flat-hierarchy modes of production seem to encourage a close-to-the-ground efficiency.

One of the questions most often asked about 9/11 is "Where was the CIA?" Why didn't they warn us? The question is more potent if phrased: "Where were the moles?" In light of the CIA's past with BCCI, ISI, the Taliban, and Al Qaeda, it's unfathomable that the CIA would completely sever ties with entities who had gained the nuclear bomb and were running international terror operations. Randy Glass's State Department contacts confirm that the State Department knew "all about planes flying into buildings." How? Well, remember that U.S. intel's job is to infiltrate our enemies, create assets, turn their spies over to our side, and create moles in enemy intelligence. U.S. intel gets an annual budget of $40 billion, there's a lot of money floating around. The right chunk of change in the right hands can prove very influential. On 9/11, the moles were in place, reporting to their handlers.

Let me state outright what others have only implied: It's probable that Mohamed Atta was some kind of double agent.

He fits the profile: the cover story, the clearance, the multiple forms of ID, and the protection. He was working both sides, and he clearly didn't know exactly what he was doing. He was "compartmentalized."[37] He was used. He was told to do his part, and that everything would follow.

The 9/11 Commission Report found that Atta swore an oath of allegiance to Osama bin Laden. Hopsicker found that he wore a Palestinian pendant around his neck and referred to Palestine as the "homeland." The allegiances to the oppressed, the "homeland," won out in the end. Atta made a choice to die for a cause. He made the ultimate sacrifice, hoping it wouldn't be in vain. Atta became one of the most famous mass-murderers, when he took three thousand innocent lives with him. In a cruel irony, his vicious martyrdom ended up benefiting the side he had abandoned. When he flew Flight 11 into One World Trade Center, he

37 The term "compartmentalized" describes to the practice of not letting any one operative on an intelligence mission know the entire operation.

thought he was doing the Islamic cause a big favor. Just the opposite was true.

When I had Daniel Hopsicker on "INN World Report," we did the first broadcast on national television of an interview with Amanda Keller. She said that Atta's close friends were German and Austrian citizens, "Peter, Stephen, and Juergen." They flew in from Hamburg to join Amanda and Atta on a three-day coke binge in Key West. Then there was a meeting with a mysterious man who arrived in a small plane. After the meeting, Amanda remembers that Atta and the Germans were morbid and morose.

Exactly who those Germans were is outside the scope of this book. But just as this work was about to go to press, Stephen Verhaaren of Naples, Florida filed a $15 thousand defamation suit against Daniel Hopsicker. Daniel identified Stephen Verhaaren, a flight school owner, as the "Stephen" Amanda Keller mentions. I spoke with Verhaaren and he denied ever knowing Atta. Verhaaren has recently been visited by the German equivalent of the FBI and claims he would no longer be in this country if Hopsicker's allegations were true. So for now, the jury is still out on Verhaaren's identity. Hopsicker, for his part, is certain that Amanda identified Verhaaren by his full name. This is going to be an interesting trial.

In May 2000, Atta got his U.S. entry visa from the U.S. Embassy in Berlin, an institution known for more than just straight diplomacy. According to Israeli spy Ben-Menashe, the Berlin Embassy was used to slip Iranian operatives into the U.S. in 1980, when Ben-Menashe witnessed George H.W. Bush and William Casey participating in secret meetings to delay the release of Iranian hostages.[38] The Berlin U.S. Embassy also may have been behind a 1986 disco bombing which created the pretext for Reagan's attack on Libya.[39]

Not only did Atta have multiple passports, he had multiple identities, occasionally using "Mohamed Arajaki," other times his full name, "Mohamed Atta El-Amir," or just "Mohamed Elamir." Mohamed Atta's email list included aviation and defense contractor personnel, including the Canadian firm Virtual Prototypes, which helped develop the avionics for F-15, F-22, and B-2.

Mohamed Atta graduated from International Officers School at Maxwell Air Force Base, Alabama, according to multiple sources in the mainstream media.[40] The media dropped the story when the Air Force said that there were probably two different Mohamed Attas. Hopsicker called up the Air Force and

38 Ari Ben-Menashe, *Profits of War: Inside the Secret U.S.-Israeli Arms Network* (New York: Sheridan Square Press, 1992.) "It means that less than ten percent of the Reagan and Bush administration double-dealing was ever revealed."–Namebase.org
39 "German TV exposes CIA, Mossad links to 1986 Berlin disco bombing." August 27, 1998 http://www.wsws.org/news/1998/aug1998/bomb1-a27.shtml
40 E.g.: *LA Times* 9/15/01, *Washington Post*, 9/16/01, Gannett News Service, 9/17/01.

demanded the other Atta's birthday, but he was refused any information. The Maxwell records department bluntly discouraged him from further curiosity. But the fact that Atta graduated from International Officers School becomes especially relevant when we study the double agent Ali Mohamed. It's one thing to speculate that Atta may have been recruited as a mole while training at a U.S. military facility. But Ali Mohamed was certainly recruited as an Egyptian double agent and then installed at a U.S. military facility, as I'll demonstrate below.

Four of the other hijackers also enjoyed high-level training at U.S. military bases; for example, Abdulaziz al-Omari attended the Aerospace Medical School at Brooks Air Force Base in Texas, and Saeed al-Ghamdi was at the Defense Language Institute at the Presidio in Monterey, California. The Defense Language Institute is especially noteworthy, because Vice Chancellor for Student Affairs Lieutenant Colonel Steve Butler was suspended after publishing a letter in June 2002 that included this declamation: "Of course Bush knew about the impending attacks on America. He did nothing to warn the American people because he needed this war on terrorism." Contacted by investigator Mike Ruppert, Butler later denied having any direct contact with Saeed al-Ghamdi, per se. (But it's noteworthy that Steve Butler was a Lieutenant Colonel in the Air Force while Francis "Frank" X. Taylor was director of the Office of Investigations at the Air Force, a post he held until July 2001.)

DOUBLE AGENT PRECEDENTS

No one has looked backward to some stark precedents. There are two men that the government and the critics all agree were double agents: Ali Mohamed and Emad Salem. You can count on one hand the amount of good material available on both these shadowy figures.

One of the many sins of omission of *The 9/11 Commission Report* was that their historical analysis started arbitrarily at 1996. Here's what they're missing: the 1993 World Trade Center bombing which left in its wake key operator Ramzi Yousef who swore someday to finish the job. Perhaps the Commission is reluctant to look at the 1993 bombing because the perpetrators in '93 were heavily infiltrated and influenced by federal informants and double agents. In fact, according to audio recordings from the period, one of the FBI's paid informants told his FBI handler that the FBI itself built the 1993 bomb.

I've been friendly with independent journalist Paul DeRienzo for a good number of years. While at WBAI radio in 1994, he walked into the office one morning to find audiotapes left for him by an anonymous visitor. The tapes were of Emad Salem, an Egyptian who had infiltrated the Jersey City mosque of the blind Sheik Omar Abdel-Rahman. Salem had been recruited by a "street-tough" Texan FBI agent named Nancy Floyd. Well before the '93 bombing, Salem got very close, very quickly, to the Sheikh. But then Floyd's higher-up at the FBI, Carson Dunbar, squashed the case. He started treating Salem like a stepchild, threatening to blow his cover, and putting Salem's life and family at risk.

Salem quit. But before he did, he told Nancy Floyd, "Don't call me when the bombs go off."[41]

Emad Salem

Emad Salem was known to make tapes of every phone conversation he had, even when calling his bank or his psychic. The tapes Paul DeRienzo discovered record Emad Salem speaking with FBI Special Agent John Anticev, after the bombing. Emad was being recruited back into the fold, but this time, he wanted ten times as much money.

Paul DeRienzo reported that, on this tape, "Salem refers to his and the Bureau's involvement in making the bomb that blew up the World Trade Center. As Salem is pressing for money while emphasizing his value as a Bureau asset, the conversation moves in and out of references to the bombing and the FBI's knowledge of the bomb making."

DeRienzo published the audio recording on his website, pdr.autono.net. Here's a key excerpt:

ANTICEV, FBI: You got paid regularly for good information. I mean the expenses were a little bit out of the ordinary and it was really questioned. Don't tell Nancy I told you this.

SALEM: Well, I have to tell her, of course.

FBI: Well then, if you have to, you have to.

SALEM: Yeah, I mean because the lady was being honest, and I was being honest, and everything was submitted with receipts, and now it's questionable.

FBI: It's not questionable, it's like a little out of the ordinary.

SALEM: OK. I don't think it was. If that what you think guys, fine, but I don't think that because we was start already building the bomb

41 Peter Lance, *Cover Up: What the Government Is Still Hiding About the War on Terror,* (New York: Regan 2004)

The Big Wedding:

which is went off in the World Trade Center. It was built by supervising supervision from the Bureau and the DA, and we was all informed about it and we know what the bomb start to be built. By who? By your confidential informant. What a wonderful great case! And then he put his head in the sand I said, "Oh, no, no, that's not true, he is son of a bitch." (Deep breath) OK. It's built with a different way in another place and that's it.

FBI: No, don't make any rash decisions. I'm just trying to be as honest with you as I can.

SALEM: Of course, I appreciate that.

If you stick with it and listen to the entire audio file on DeRienzo's site, there's a dramatic moment at the end, when John Anticev seems to show his hand. Wondering why Anticev didn't contradict Salem when Salem accused the FBI of "building the bomb" with the "supervision of the Bureau"?

Perhaps because the 1993 bombing was a dry run to see if an attack on the World Trade Center could happen and be covered up under the auspices of the FBI and other intelligence groups. Anticev was OK with what happened, he reassured Salem (and himself?) that:

> "We're doing this for a higher reason. We know what we're doing and we know what it's gonna mean in the future. Forget about bureaucrats! Forget about them. They come and go, OK? We know what we're doing, and at the end we're gonna at least be able to look at each other and say we tried the best we could, ya know? Not for the government. The 'government' is this very, you know, what do you call, unidentifiable thing, you know? It's a, sometimes it's one person affecting you, sometimes it's bureaucratic things, but we'll still know what we did. That's all we're gonna say."[42]

ALI MOHAMED

The CIA actually admitted that they were "partly culpable" for the first World Trade Center bombing, according to an internal report quietly produced after the fact. The report was only mentioned in a British newspaper.[43] Although some researchers attribute FBI Special Agent Carson Dunbar's hostility to Salem to be a lack of savvy, it's more likely that he was following orders from above. Dunbar had been very active in the witch-hunt and railroading of FBI whistle-blower Richard Taus in the late '80s. Taus was the first to discover a CIA-linked Oliver North front

42 *The Shadow* (New York), "Shadow Exclusive: FBI Bombed World Trade Center" issue #34. A full audio recording of the Salem/Anticev exchange is available at DeRienzo's website— http://nwo.media.xs2.net/tape/SalemWBAI.mp3

43 Andrew Marshall, "Terror 'Blowback' Burns CIA: America's spies paid and trained their nation's worst enemies," *The Independent* (UK), November 1, 1998: "A confidential CIA internal survey concluded that it was 'partly culpable' for the World Trade Center bomb, according to reports at the time. There had been blowback."

group in Long Island, New York. When he refused to look the other way, regarding this group (the "Freeport K-Team") he was sent away for a record-breaking thirty-two to ninety years on unsubstantiated charges of pedophilia.

It's refreshingly honest of the CIA to admit part-culpability in the 1993 Trade Center bombing. Not only is it commendable, it's hard to consider them not admitting some guilt, given the fact that they had worked closely before the bombing with an Egyptian double agent named Ali Mohamed. Mohamed was a Major in the Egyptian Army, and, through a military exchange program, a sergeant with the U.S. He taught special operations at Fort Bragg, and was closely associated with the Green Berets, Delta Force, and other elite tactical units. He worked as an informant for the FBI, CIA, and testified for the prosecution in the trial of blind Sheik Omar Abdel-Rahman.

Before the 1993 World Trade Center bombing, Ali Mohamed

Carson Dunbar, ex-FBI, now with New Jersey State Troopers

was making regular trips from Fort Bragg, North Carolina to Jersey City, where he trained four of the key players in the bombing. One of his men, El Sayyid Nosair, assassinated Rabbi Meir Kahane of the Far-Right Jewish Defense League, in a hotel in Manhattan. Nosair's apartment was raided and forty-six cases of documents were booked into evidence. Yet NYPD Chief of Detectives, Joseph Berelli, told the *Village Voice* that they found "nothing that would stir your imagination," that Nosair was a "lone, deranged gunman," and, "we can't connect anyone else to the Kahane shooting."[44] A member of Egyptian Islamic Jihad, Ali Mohamed played a key role in the 1998 U.S. Embassy bombings in Africa. He took the photos that enabled Osama bin Laden to know where to send the truck bombs.

Ali Mohamed's case is perplexing—why was he allowed to operate for so long? The guy had such juice that when he was busted in Canada with an Al Qaeda terrorist in 1993, he had the authorities call the FBI. That single phone call sprang him from prison[45].

Although Ali Mohamed was technically convicted in relation to his role in the 1998 African Embassy bombings, no one is exactly sure where he's being held. Or if he's being held.

Some speculate that Ali was let out a back door in order to go back to spying on the terrorists he gets along with so well. The August 6, 2001 Presidential Daily Brief is partly based on

44 From original interviews with Peter Dale Scott, Ph.D., and Peter Lance.
45 Estanislao Oziewicz and Tu Thanh Ha "Canada Freed Top Al Qaeda Operative" *Globe and Mail* (Toronto), 22 November 2001

The Big Wedding:

intelligence from "an Egyptian Islamic Jihad operative." For all we know, that operative could be working with Ali Mohamed, back on the street, and working both sides.

Emad Salem and Ali Mohamed are both highly
trained operatives and both display fierce dedication
to principles, even amid shifting loyalties. Before his
death, Mohamed Atta shared all these attributes. Atta
was not unnoticed when he trained in Florida. Israeli

Ali Mohamed

intelligence had an entire field office dispatched to the area, in
disguise. Posing as "art students," over one hundred young
Mossad agents kept tabs on Mohamed Atta and Marwan Al-
Shehhi, following them from Hamburg, Germany to Hollywood,
Florida throughout 2000 and 2001. In August 2001, the Israelis
were discovered by U.S. authorities and quietly ejected from the
country.

In response, on August 23, 2001, Mossad published a list of
names, warning that nineteen potential terrorists were planning an imminent attack on the USA. Only then did the CIA tell
the State Department, FBI, and INS to put two names on the
terrorist watch list. The CIA had observed these two terrorists,
Khalid Almihdhar and Nawaf Alhazmi, at a Malaysian terrorist
conference in 2000 and believed they were linked to the bombing
of the USS Cole. Both helped take over Flight 77 on 9/11. Yet
Almihdhar and Alhazmi were allowed to board the flight and
crash it into the Pentagon. The CIA was reluctant to hassle
these terrorists and only identified them in August 2001 because
the Mossad embarrassed them into it.[46]

On August 31, Egyptian President Hosni Mubarak warned
the United States of an imminent attack. Based on Egyptian
moles inside Al Qaeda, Mubarak said he knew of the plot and
passed along the intelligence. "We expected that something was
going to happen and informed the Americans. We told them."[47]

THE TAUS/FAROOQ CONNECTION

Let's return to the case of Richard Taus, the
FBI agent who was sent away for crimes he
didn't commit by the notoriously corrupt New
York FBI field office. For standing up to Bush,
Oliver North, and their covert criminal corrup-
tion, Taus has been locked down in Clinton

*Richard Taus,
in better times.*

46 German press reports on CIA surveillance of the "Hamburg Cell" and Mossad obser-
vation of Atta in Florida, Oct. 5, 2002 a news posting and analysis by 9/11 researcher
Nick Levis, who supplied, translated, and deconstructed three sources: (1) *Der Spiegel*,
Oct. 1, 2002 (2) *Die Zeit*, Oct. 3, 2002 (3) *Berliner Zeitung*, Sept. 24, 2001
47 Associated Press, 'Egypt Leader Says He Warned America,' December 7, 2001.

Correctional Maximum Security in upstate New York near the Canadian border. We've been in correspondence since 2001. I now own a twenty-pound stack of documents that relate to his case. (I'm convinced that his story and his liberation will make a great project for the right bunch of dedicated activists in the near future.)

On 9/11, Taus was approached by his cellmate, a Pakistani-born CIA agent, named Mian Farooq. Farooq was familiar enough with the 9/11 attack to be able to tell Taus that Atta was the team leader. He shared this info with Taus on the morning of 9/11, before the news media announced Atta's name. Farooq knew Mohamed Atta personally. They met when Farooq was stationed at a job inside U.S. Customs at JFK Airport, New York City. Taus told me Farooq remembers in 1996 Atta showed up in

> "the uniform of an airline pilot. Atta explained...that his uniform appearance was due to his ownership in a Florida-based flight school. Farooq further noted that Atta became increasingly hostile toward the Unites States, particularly after Atta's divorce from his American wife of German/Irish descent. The couple had three children."

If this is true, it means that Amanda Keller was not a dalliance, but part of a larger predilection Atta had for women of German/Aryan/Northern European heritage. Amanda corroborated that Atta had very Westernized kids. Hopsicker reported Atta's son lived in France and loved the Beastie Boys.

Why did Farooq tell Taus what he knew about Atta? The Pakistani said he no longer trusted his handlers at CIA, and felt that the FBI was the "right authority" to share information with about 9/11. In exchange, two agents from the local FBI office arrived and swiftly proved him wrong. They called Taus names, and so frustrated Farooq that the Pakistani source refused to talk to them. Taus wrote a letter to then-Attorney General Ashcroft, which I reprint here in Appendix I (page 157). After the FBI burnt the source, the CIA got in touch with Farooq and told him to zip it, or else.

If Farooq's information can be verified, then it makes 1996 a year of serious significance for Atta. Farooq remembers him in New York City bragging about an ownership stake in a Florida flight school. In Hamburg that same year, Atta began putting together his cell, organizing and recruiting the team out of the Muslim community that gathered at Al Kuds mosque.

CHAPTER 5:

WILDCARD!
ACROSS CANADA WITH
DELMART VREELAND

It's August, 2002 and I'm in Toronto.

Delmart Vreeland wants to meet me in the parking lot of the Loblaw grocery store on Lake Shore Drive. I arrive as a silver Lincoln circles the parking garage. I park and the car silently glides to me. The passenger door opens. Vreeland is sitting in back, hair cropped short into a Caesar cut, wearing a tight black ribbed t-shirt and black parachute pants. He looks like Eminem. He leans forward and says, "Lock your car. Get in."

As a black storm builds out in the harbor, we head to a big tourist restaurant called Docks. Vreeland buys us two beers each; we drink and talk outside on the deck. He wonders aloud if anyone is tailing us. Suddenly, everyone around me is middle-aged, dressed inconspicuously, and wearing sunglasses. The storm breaks and we run inside. The middle-aged men follow us, still wearing their sunglasses.

That night, the Lincoln takes me, Vreeland, Vreeland's son, and the son's best friend up north to a resort lodge. Vreeland feels safer there. He says he's buying a condo for $600 thousand in one lump sum to be wired over. From where? He won't say. Does it have to do with his work with former U.S. Treasury operatives, people who claim to be attempting to recover over $27.6 trillion lost in 1993 when a secret Israeli/Palestinian peace deal went awry? (Yes, that's right, $27.6 trillion.)

Vreeland's story begins in December 2000, when he was arrested in Toronto and charged by Canadian authorities with fraud, obstructing a peace officer, and making a death threat. The Canadian charges were soon dropped to speed his extradition back to the U.S., where he was wanted in numerous states on charges that include identity and financial fraud, forgery, and battery to an officer. It's a long list, but in person, Vreeland is unfazed.

"I've seen other lists, with even more, hundreds of them, and then I've also seen them disappear. Remember, the FBI/NSIC fingerprints came back negative." It's true that when he was arrested in Canada, according to the arresting officer's notes, the FBI said they had no fingerprints on the guy.

Vreeland told Canadian authorities he was a spy for the Office of Naval Intelligence (ONI), one of the oldest and most powerful intelligence arms of the U.S. government. He also claimed that, if he were extradited to the US, he would be killed. Why? Vreeland appears to have been exposed to some level of government foreknowledge about 9/11.

While in prison during the summer of 2001, Vreeland and his attorneys repeatedly attempted to warn the world about imminent terrorist attacks. Vreeland's then-attorney Rocco Galati, a respected former Canadian prosecutor known for his support of progressive causes, made what he called "head-bashing attempts"[48] to have Vreeland put in touch with the proper authorities, to pass on "vital information about national security"[49] to the governments of Canada and the US. Sometime around August 11 or 12, Vreeland wrote a set of notes. They listed a number of potential terrorist targets including the Sears Towers, World Trade Center, White House, and Pentagon. The notes included the language, "Let one happen. Stop the rest!!!"

48 Kathleen Harris, "Diplomat's Death Remains Unsolved; What Killed Him: A Thief, Natural Causes, or Cloak-and-Dagger?" *The Ottawa Sun* December 9, 2001.
49 Ibid.

Here's the whole note:

Navy ???
Sears tower ? chicago
World trade Centre
white House —
pentagon ?
world bank Malaise
water supplies —
Scotia bank/Toronto
Parliament Bldg. attawa —
Royal Bank Toronto or ????.

— ??? will paint me crazy and call me a liar —

???? lets one happen — stop the rest !!!

NATES: Bar lake | LIAN cHamber / MALA:SIA | Bilateral
MKY — CHALVA TURBINSKY | Zantria — Browen nuclear | arma/techn — exchange
OLEG | ubiate petrasska | (Soft Rite 1 and 2.) WHY Bank ?
? MARC | world Trall Centre (DR. HAIDEC)? 2007 2009
Tcom HENREY | in Lux — CCH / WP — Pentagon or ???House ?
— Bio / NMH
OTTAWA - F.M. R / Boston | Ned | disaster — Brown RecLuse
DOCKS - fea — VLADIVOSTOK / Kiev | WATER / How ?
M234 Raq Kuwait E, purgable | WT as pts contacts

— No comments on letter — No Thankyou, No comment —
Transfer to ottawa, Ned custody, Safe here or Mr Bree — or
my own private apt — My Expense — Ned JO

C/R - Coo agreement 76-97

The name "bin Laden" appears at the top of the central paragraph. It mentions a list of targets: "White House...World Trade Center...Pentagon...let one happen, stop the rest...prob. they will call me crazy."

Vreeland sealed these notes in an envelope and handed them to his Canadian jailers. His lawyers, Galati and Paul Slansky, another well-known former Canadian prosecutor, introduced the documents into court that October. For their efforts, they were harassed with dead cats hung on their porches and smashed car windows. Galati later bowed out of all cases having to do with international figures linked to terrorism.

News of Vreeland spread quickly when alternative 9/11 journalist Mike Ruppert began sending back dramatic dispatches from the courtroom in Toronto. Recalling Jefferson Airplane's hallucinogenic visions, Ruppert called Vreeland a "white knight talking backward"[50] in articles published on his site, Copvcia.com, and on GNN.tv. To Ruppert, Vreeland's story became something of an Internet phenomenon, with thousands of readers around the world tracking every dramatic twist and turn. His long, colorful list of outstanding warrants in the U.S. was released to the public, and the international man of mystery was dismissed by some as a two-bit con man who had concocted an elaborate yarn to avoid prosecution. Leading the charge was Terry Weems, Vreeland's vindictive half brother. Canadian authorities dropped their charges against Vreeland on March 14, 2002, and he was paroled to house arrest, waiting for an extradition hearing.

His case might have slipped off the radar completely, but in March, 2002, *The Nation's* Washington correspondent David Corn published an article entitled "September 11 X-Files."[51] The article lumped Georgia Congresswoman Cynthia McKinney, the French book that claimed a plane didn't hit the Pentagon, and Vreeland supporter Ruppert into the same "kook" category. Corn claimed that their "misguided" efforts to look for a conspiracy at the top distracted the public from the more important work of analyzing the Bush administration's real "political" misdeeds, as if 9/11 was an apolitical event. Corn wrote that Vreeland "was no spy, he was a flim-flammer," and characterized Ruppert as a web surfer with a vivid imagination: "Ruppert is no journalist." Ruppert fired back, and hundreds of his supporters wrote Corn and *The Nation* in protest. Corn's response was to intensify his attack, publishing "To Protect And To Spin," a scathing profile of Ruppert full of personal details, including romantic affairs gone awry and other personal nadirs.

50 The actual lyrics to the Jefferson Airplane song "White Rabbit" are themselves a fine summary of Vreeland's situation in Canada at the time:
    When the men on the chess board get up and tell you where to go/And you've just had some kind of mushroom, and your mind is moving low/Go ask Alice. I think she'll know./When logic and proportion have fallen sloppy dead, And the white knight is talking backward/and the red queen's off with her head/Remember what the door - mouse said: "Feed your head! Feed your head!"

51 *The Nation,* "September 11 X-Files" March 30, 2002

Partly in response to what he felt were threatening attacks from Toronto radio hosts on CKLN, in the spring of 2002 Vreeland developed his own site, ltvreeland.com. He posted information about his case, court documents, and records of financial transactions involving a certain former Reagan White House operative named Leo Wanta. (The site disappeared in December 2003.)

On May 21, 2002, the plot thickened, when the FBI's Coleen Rowley publicly accused FBI director Robert Mueller of hampering crucial investigations into alleged 9/11 conspirators. There was a "delicate and subtle shading/skewing of facts by [Mueller] and others at the highest levels of FBI management...The term 'cover-up' would be too strong a characterization, which is why I am attempting to carefully (and perhaps over-laboriously) choose my words here." Rowley pointed out that FBI headquarters' refusal to approve a FISA warrant to search the laptop of Zacharias Moussaoui was unprecedented.

Around the same time as Coleen Rowley's story broke the news, the "Phoenix Memo" came to light. It had been authored in July 2001, by Arizona-based FBI Special Agent Ken Williams and it called on FBI leadership to investigate potential terrorists training at U.S. flight schools. The Rowley and Williams memos appeared as German, Egyptian, Russian, and Israeli intelligence services claimed they had warned the White House that a specific attack was imminent.

The allegations of Russian intelligence foreknowledge is especially relevant to Vreeland's case. Vreeland got his information about 9/11 on a trip to Moscow, working as an armed courier of diplomatic documents. According to a September 12, 2001 story by Russian newspaper *Izvestia*, "Yesterday at the headquarters of Central Intelligence Service in Langley, a confidential meeting between one of the Deputy Directors of CIA and a special messenger of Russian Intelligence Service took place. According to NewsRu sources, he delivered to his American colleagues some documents including audio tapes with telephone conversations directly relating to terrorist attacks on Washington and New York last Tuesday. *According to these sources, Russian Intelligence agents know the organizers and executors of these terrorist attacks. More than that, Moscow warned Washington about preparation to these actions a couple of weeks before they happened."* [italics mine]

The last two sentences of that lead paragraph were later deleted from the Izvestia website, but not before they were archived by Mike Ruppert's staff.

If Russian intelligence knew of 9/11 beforehand, then it's possible Vreeland did run into that information in Moscow. On September 18, Eleanor Hill, staff director of the Joint Inquiry into 9/11, testified that there were no less than twelve separate warnings about terrorists hijacking planes in the last four years, including, contrary to the Bush administration's previous statements, at least one that specifically involved crashing a plane into the World Trade Center.

Could Delmart Vreeland, extensive criminal record and all, be another U.S. intelligence operative who blew the whistle before the 9/11 tragedy? When you place Vreeland next to Randy Glass and consider the startling similarities to their cases, you realize that it's the guys from the street, the guys who have been raped and discarded who are the ones with nothing to lose. This is no hyperbole; Vreeland was literally raped in prison. He and Glass were blowing the whistle on 9/11 throughout the summer of 2001.

I spent six months researching Vreeland. I went where the investigation lead me. At the end, the story included top Clinton White House intelligentsia, late-White House lawyer Vince Foster, pardoned arms dealer Marc Rich, "Reagan's junkyard dog" Ambassador Leo Wanta, a shady Russian tycoon, and a country-western musician half-brother of Vreeland's with a seemingly inexhaustible vendetta to have Vreeland sent to prison.

Delmart Vreeland is a liar and an accomplished con man, adept at spinning tales and manipulating allegiances to further his own goals. His critics were half right: Vreeland is crooked. In other words, he is the perfect candidate for work in U.S. intelligence.

DISSECTING THE NOTE

Vreeland claims the now-infamous notes were part of a thirty-seven-page memo to Admiral Vern Clark, Chief of Naval Operations. Although they fast developed a reputation as a "warning letter," Vreeland says this wasn't his intention. As Vreeland told me in our first interview on April 6, 2002, "These are my own personal notes...The only way to understand the whole thing is to read the whole memo. We have not made that public yet. A big YET on that."

I asked Vreeland about the exact contents and codes of the

note:

What were you trying to do in August 2001?

"I wanted to avert 9/11."

If you had five minutes with President Bush what would you say?

"I could not tell you what I would say to him. I am forbidden from telling you. I am not suspecting him. I am not making a statement...I am not doing any Bush-bashing."

Are you afraid?

"I'm surprised I'm still here. I got too many people wanting me dead. If I was after me, I would kidnap me, I would drug me, I would get the info I wanted, and then I would kill me."

If you were after you, do you think you could get you?

"Absolutely! I can get anyone if I wanted them badly enough."

What information would you shake out of yourself?

"I'd want to know where the Wanta money is right now. Who in the Pentagon has done wrong? Who killed who...black ops...illegal arms trades, where are blueprints, the docs you brought back from Moscow? Where's Susanna at? Was it her or Oleg who poisoned Bastien? And did McComb County give up Bobby Moore intentionally? Who shot Foster? Canadian spy Marc."

"Susanna" and "Oleg" may be references to the Russian contacts Bastien was known to have in his hotel room shortly before his body was found. "Bobby Moore" we will meet below, and "Foster" is a reference to Clinton White House attorney Vince Foster.

According to his sworn affidavit, when Vreeland was arrested in Canada on December 6, 2000, he contacted the Canadian Security Intelligence Service (CSIS), Canada's equivalent to the CIA. When the CSIS didn't respond, his claims about being ONI were laughed off by the Royal Canadian Mounted Police. The laughter stopped that summer when he was able to shed light on the mysterious death of Marc Bastien, a Canadian "diplomat" in Moscow. Vreeland wrote Bastien a letter in June 2001, but when CSIS informed him that Bastien had died six months earlier in December 2000 from "natural causes," Vreeland started making noise. The official explanation soon changed. Bastien didn't commit suicide. Vreeland was right. Vreeland claims Bastien was the Canadian intelligence contact he met in Moscow. "I knew stuff about Bastien that no one else did."

When did you leave Office of Naval Intelligence?

"1998."

Why?

"The opportunity came, I was getting old, I don't like getting shot, getting stabbed."

Vreeland's note contains the scrawl "Dr. Haider-> who's his contacts?" According to the *L.A. Times,* Dr. Haider is an alias of Amar Makhnulif, a.k.a. Abu Doha, a key Al Qaeda figure accused of being part of a plan to blow up the Los Angeles airport on New Year's Eve 2000. Abu Doha was arrested in London by British authorities in February of 2001, but was then mysteriously released.

In April, Vreeland told me, "I don't believe Osama had a fucking thing to do with 9/11. I don't believe he set it up. I don't believe it was his people."

In our interview in September 2002, Vreeland's beliefs hadn't changed. He asked, "Why would an agent of the U.S. government blow up the WTC? You've got Putin pissed off at Afghanistan, you've got the U.S. training Osama...the document in Russian talks about blowing up things in the U.S." Earlier, in an April 17 interview with popular Yahoo! radio host Jeff Rense, Vreeland said that in Moscow he had read "a letter from Iraq to Moscow detailing what would happen." Rense asked him "How specific was that letter?" Vreeland responded evenly, "Quite specific. Except for the day. It said September, World Trade Center. It specifically named that target. Then it identified what was to happen after."

THE WORLD'S BEST CON MAN

It's Saturday morning in "cottage country" at a lodge about one hundred miles north of Toronto. The lake is as big as the sky and opens up right under my window. I go down to Vreeland's room for bagels and talk about his criminal past.

"If you're the world's best con man, you're not going to work for yourself, are you?" he says. "That would be stupid. Who would you want to work for? Someone who can protect you."

Discussing his extensive criminal record, he repeatedly claims, "I've never been legally convicted of anything." The vocal emphasis is on "legally," by which Vreeland seems to mean "legitimately." The alleged crimes were just part of his cover, "I played the criminal. Like taking down [a] drug dealer...we needed information, I would get arrested and put in the same cell as him. I needed to have a criminal record...it's easy to make someone your friend. I can become friends with suits, punkers, rastas, anyone."

Although he is accused of credit card fraud in Michigan, Vreeland's credit report states that he never had a credit card.

The Nation's Corn called Vreeland's note "a hard-to-decipher collection of phrases and names" that "holds no specific information related to the 9/11 assaults. There is no date mentioned, no obvious reference to a set of perpetrators."

The distortion Corn is guilty of here is right out of the tactics of his disinformation-master hero, Ted Shackley. Shackley was the CIA station chief who ran anti-Castro terror operations into Cuba in the early '60s and presided over CIA-approved heroin trafficking in Laos during Vietnam. Corn wrote a generously admiring book about Shackley called *Blond Ghost*.

According to Greta Knutzen, reporting from Toronto for FromTheWilderness.com, "Vreeland requested that his guards seal the note and register it in his personal effects, which they did." As of her report several months ago, "The fact that the note was written and sealed a month prior to the violent attacks of Sept. 11 has not been disputed." However, a phone call to the Canadian prosecution team resulted in new, somewhat murky results. When I asked Assistant DA Dorette Hugins to confirm that the prosecution didn't dispute that the note was handed to the jailers in mid-August 2001, she immediately said, "Yes, it is true." A minute later, after speaking with someone in her office, she changed her answer to "No, the prosecution now thinks he got the notes to the jailers after 9/11." A forensics test would have answered this question in court, but the Canadians didn't want to keep Vreeland around that long.

Dorette Hugins and lead prosecutor Kevin Wilson have their hands full trying to negate strong evidence that Vreeland has some kind of U.S. intelligence connection. On January 10, defense attorney Paul Slansky called the Pentagon from a speakerphone in court, and was able to receive Lieutenant Delmart Vreeland's office number and phone extension. The prosecution desperately tried to explain that one by claiming Vreeland is a hacker who discovered a way to access the Pentagon's mainframe from jail. Discussing this that morning at the lodge, Vreeland was incredulous: "You can track an IP [Internet Protocol address] in a heartbeat. Why haven't I been prosecuted for this? That's so stupid."

Vreeland and I are sitting out on the balcony of his hotel room in the crisp Canadian sunshine. This trip is showing me a side of Vreeland that I hadn't seen. He has a seventeen-year-old "son" he is very protective of. For this article, I promised to change his name. Call him "Joey."

Joey is a punk raver in bellbottoms with millions of pockets. He chain-smokes, and talks incessantly about being drunk and how dad's connections are going to get him into Harvard Law School. Vreeland and Joey are endlessly bickering and scrapping, and then bumming Players Navy Cut cigarettes off each other. Just as often as smoking them, Joey will throw the cigarettes at his father in exasperation. Vreeland claims to never have hit Joey, but he does often grab him, and is extremely physical with him, a strange, uncertain mix of roughhousing and desperate attempts at disciplining an uncontrollable kid.

Or maybe there's something going on between Vreeland and Joey.

Later, the guys at CKLN radio disputed that the thirty-five-year-old Vreeland really had a seventeen-year-old son. Reflecting on Vreeland three years after I first met him, it's becoming more likely that Vreeland may have been the victim of childhood sexual abuse. And CKLN might have been right about something they suggested when I met with them in Toronto: Vreeland may be a pedophile.

Vreeland's slippery psyche seems to be suffering from a split personality disorder, a fugue state eerily similar to that of Paul Bonacci, Lee Harvey Oswald, Sirhan Sirhan, and Mohamed Atta. Three years after originally reporting on Vreeland for the upstart Guerrilla News Network, I've been exposed to some of the most "out-there" data on GOP tactics and sexual behavior. Vreeland's story may be a part of that larger story. Although it's not normally discussed in "respectable" circles, there's a documented history of a program informally called the "Monarch Program." It is something of a descendent of the CIA's MK-ULTRA mind-control experiments in the '50s and '60s. The Monarch Program seeks to create assassins, covert operatives, and sexual playthings out of society's most vulnerable individuals. It seeks to study how victims of childhood sexual trauma are then manipulable.

In 2005, the Bush White House suffered a scandal when it was discovered that credentialed White House Press Corps guest reporter Jeff Gannon was actually a hired call boy.

The scandal broke, dissipated, and the mass media never really understood its implications.

Savvier researchers thought that the Gannon scandal might finally expose the GOP-linked pedophilia cult lurking in the shadowier circles of both Bush presidencies and the Republican Party since June 1989. In 1989, a call boys ring in the Bush White House made the front page of the *Washington*

Times, and then disappeared. It's one of the unreported realities of the Bush world that exposes a lot of deep, repressed homosexual energy. But the feasting on young children is the unforgivable part. It's the ultimate abuse of power and it smacks of a deep, fascistic, pagan brutality. Locked inside the Bush family's heart of hearts there lies this little scandal that so far the handlers have been adept at covering up. The exception is an excellent, self-published book called *The Franklin Cover-Up,* by former Nebraska State Senator John W. DeCamp. In 1993, a BBC-affiliated team made a serious TV documentary, based on original research and DeCamp's book. The documentary was titled "Conspiracy of Silence." Due to mysterious political pressure, "Conspiracy" was never broadcast, despite its scheduled debut May 3, 1994, which had been announced, and advertised on the Discovery Channel.

Long-term observers of Vreeland think that he was abused as a child, perhaps programmatically. His multiple-reality mix of truth and lies is something akin to the multiple personality disorders of the victims of childhood sexual abuse like Paul Bonacci. In *Franklin Cover-Up* and "Conspiracy of Silence" we met the personable Bonacci, a former Boys Town, Nebraska orphan. Bonacci relates how he was forced to be a hustler/plaything at GOP parties in Georgetown frequented by the Washington elite throughout the mid and late '80s. Bush White House aide Craig Spence arranged midnight tours of the White House for the boys. At the parties in Georgetown, they were forced to allow older Republican men to put heated gourds up their rectums. At parties in the woods, boys were shot in the head and then sodomized. Needless to say, when the story broke in the cagey *Washington Times,* the Bush White House's Craig Spence feared a "doublecross" by the CIA. He was soon found dead in a DC hotel room.

In the midst of an unsuccessful attempt to get the rambunctious Joey to respect his authority, Vreeland comments, "I don't know which is worse, getting shot at or being a dad." It's sounding more and more forced. He says "dad" like he is selling me a story. I look up at the hotel TV and a video by Nickelback comes on: "Father is a name you haven't earned yet. Kicking your ass would be a pleasure."

Among his Internet pals, Vreeland's code name is "Wildcard." Vreeland would like people to think that he can transform into anything and become as powerful as he wills, like the wild card in an amateur poker game. The nickname is apt for another reason. Vreeland's speech patterns are untamed, and he seems to be in a constant state of chemical imbalance. He drinks like there's a fire in his brain. He claims to have been given Clonapin for fifteen years by the Navy (Clonapin is a strong anti-seizure drug sometimes used to treat anxiety). He jumps from topic to topic like he's on a mix of acid and speed. In the hotel room, he tries to convince me to get people to wire over five hundred dollars so that he can go to Radio Shack, buy parts, and build us a replica of a missile defense weapon he once developed for the Navy's Nuclear Training Command.

The next day at the lodge, Joey is still trying to get his Dad's attention by trashing hotel property. He has to be rescued by a nautical patrol while kayaking with his pal, Jacob. The boys rent bikes, and ride them around inside the hotel. Vreeland yells at them. Joey drinks a beer in the hotel bar with the ID Vreeland got him so he could jet-ski. Vreeland is pissed off, and announces that we will all be leaving that night, our trip cut short. Vreeland's "Dad Story" includes a kid that has obviously not been around a parent in a long, long time. It's beginning to feel like Joey knows the story is an act, as he flaunts his ability to chain smoke and drink around his "dad." I ask Vreeland about his drinking habits. It's fine, he says, with Joey "I get totally trashed twice a week—we have an agreement."

Vreeland was trained to be an assassin, as was "Conspiracy of Silence" star witness Paul Bonacci, the White House hustler. They both were given high-end sniper target training. Jane Woodbury, Vreeland's mother, testified during the trial that she remembers Delmart repeatedly warning her not to fly, especially not to New York, throughout August 2001. Immediately after the September 11 attacks, she claims that she was visited by a U.S. Secret Service agent named Mitchell Szydlowski, who asked the bizarre question, "Do you believe Delmart is psychic? Did he ever predict 9/11 to you?" Jane Woodbury said no to both questions. In Canadian Court, the Secret Service confirmed that the visit took place. Jane Woodbury's current husband, Tony Matar, remembers her stating in the fall of 2001 that her son had predicted the attack. I called Secret Service agent Mitchell Szydlowski several times but my calls were not returned. Vreeland's attorneys submitted evidence that Jane's shop in Michigan was burglarized three times in recent months. The break-in artists were only interested in taking Vreeland's military records.

At 3:26 PM, hotel security calls. They want both boys off the property by sundown. Joey tells security he will have them all fired. The plan to leave that night is cemented. The silver Lincoln arrives and we all pile in for the trip back to Toronto.

MOSCOW NIGHTS

I asked Vreeland, "You claim to have left the ONI (Office of Naval Intelligence) in 1998, returning in 2000. Why did you come back in 2000 and go to Moscow for ONI?"

"I knew the system," Vreeland said.

Vreeland says that, upon being pulled into the Navy in 1984, he helped develop technology related to Star Wars strategic missile defense technology. Ruppert believes the Star Wars stuff is a cover story. After all, according to Vreeland's public records, he did not attend college. But then, his habeas corpus application contradicts itself about where he graduated from high school. Have Vreeland's education records been doctored? When pressed about his background in science, he answers that his reading habits consist of "Asimov, physics, whatever."

Looking over my notes from our interview three years after our 2002 interview, I notice that Vreeland boasted, "I could build a model of the Stealth Satellite System with five hundred dollars in parts from Radio Shack." In August 2002, this seemed unverifiable and a little silly. But then three months later, on December 4, National Security Archive's Jeffrey Richelson published a book, titled *The Wizards of Langley: Inside the CIA's Directorate of Science and Technology* that broke news on the ONYX stealth satellite program. The high-end reconnaissance weapon made the front page of the *Washington Post* and the *New York Times* in 2004 when Senator John Rockefeller complained of the Senate's inability to kill the program, despite having voted against it for two years.[53]

In September 2000, Vreeland claims he was sent by ONI to Russia to act as a courier for documents regarding the "Stealth Satellite System Terminator." But something went wrong for him in Moscow. Part of this mission was to break into the apartment of Chalva Tchigirinski, the Russian oil mogul.

On Vreeland's old website, audio files of old voicemails left for him at the time of his arrest leave behind an interesting trail: "Lt. Commander Tom Welsh from JAG", i.e. the military court, "Captain McCarthy," and various top brass, media, and law enforcement personnel. Then there's John Criminaro, with the U.S. Embassy in Moscow. Criminaro "tried for two hours" to

53 *Washington Post* ("New Spy Satellite Debated on Hill," 11 Dec. 2004) and *New York Times* ("New Spy Plan Said to Involve Satellite System," 12 Dec. 2004) describe a secret satellite program that the Senate intelligence committee has voted to cancel but survives in the current intelligence budget due to strong support from the House and Senate appropriations committees and the House intelligence committee -National Security Archive

send that fax. On January 7, 2001, Criminaro called Vreeland several times, but did not return multiple messages I left for him on his voice mail in Moscow. John Criminaro is with the U.S. Embassy's Office of Environment, Science, and Technology.

THE MAN FROM MICHIGAN

Delmart Vreeland was born March 20, 1966, near Grosse Pointe, Michigan, outside Detroit. He and his half-brother Terry Weems counted Steve Tocco among their close family friends (Tocco is related to Jake Tocco, the famous Detroit mafia leader.) Vreeland was not close to his father, Delmart Sr., a chef who was in prison briefly for embezzlement from the Big Boy restaurants he managed. Delmart's stepfather, Bob Woodbury, was a Detroit cop who got the thirteen-year-old Delmart part-time work for the Bureau of Alcohol, Tobacco and Firearms, busting "party stores" along Whittier Ave. that sold liquor to kids. The only problem with this arrangement is that the ATF required the arrests go on Delmart's juvenile record.

From there, Delmart Vreeland joined the Navy. The official Navy records entered into Canadian Court (and in Vreeland's habeas corpus application) claim that Vreeland was admitted on November 14, 1985, and was discharged only five months later. On March 7, 1986, it appears he was kicked out after repeated write-ups for insubordination and an unwillingness to do push-ups. But the Navy's claim about a 1986 discharge is suspect for a number of reasons. In an *LA Times* story dated October 2, 1986, "Mike Vreeland" appears as a friendly witness in a story about a massive cocaine seizure. Confidential sources within LAPD (contacted through Mike Ruppert) have confirmed that this was indeed Delmart "Mike" Vreeland, in training as a special agent of the ONI. The *Times* states that the cocaine raid was headed up by the LAPD's Lt. J.R. Schiller, long believed to have intelligence connections.[54]

On August 21, 2001, Vreeland's note was sealed and in the hands of his jailers. Vreeland knew the attack was happening some time in the next month. He called the U.S. Navy Office of Personnel Service Detachment in Norfolk, Virginia. He spoke with Petty Officer Terry Guilford. Through a three-way connection with his attorneys, he was able to make an audio recording and transcript of this conversation, submitted to court as an

54 Sources on this include Mae Brussell, the late California radio host, researcher and historian of Iran/Contra and the JFK Assassination.

The Big Wedding:

exhibit.

The petty officer cheerfully helped Vreeland confirm that the records did show him joining the Navy in 1985, only to be kicked out five months later in 1986. The records also showed Vreeland's rank as "Lieutenant," a rank that usually takes years to obtain. Petty Officer Guilford admitted that something smelled funny. Guilford suggested that perhaps Vreeland was in a "low-key type field" or got his rank through unusual means. "You're a fishy guy, sir," said Guilford, who agreed with Vreeland several times throughout the conversation that the records appeared to have been tampered with. When Vreeland confirmed Guilford's name, Guilford said, perhaps only half joking, "I don't know if I wanna tell you my name now."

I confirmed this conversation with Petty Officer Guilford on June 12, 2002. On the phone, Guilford remembered Lieutenant Vreeland from eleven months earlier. Although all of Vreeland's records came up blank on almost all of the Navy's databases, when Guilford checked Vreeland with the Defense Enrollment Eligibility Reporting System (DEERS), he was able to view a "read only" record that confirmed that Vreeland joined up in November 1985. But this time Guilford read out loud that the DEERS record showed that Vreeland was in the Navy's employ until December 9, 2000. Someone in records-keeping had changed course. Suddenly the record read closer to what Vreeland originally claimed. I double-checked this DEERS record at the local Navy/Marines recruiting station, and the exit date of year 2000 was still there.

All other medical and personnel records in the DEERS, including Vreeland's blood type, were blank. Officer Guilford found the blood type record especially odd. "It's not just that it's unknown, it just says 'blank.' That's not unusual for someone who just joined up, but it's weird for someone who's been with us for a while, fifteen years...I thought I would be able to print that, but it wouldn't print." According to the U.S. Navy's Rockie Beasley, head of the Personnel Support Department at the Norfolk Naval Base. It is not easy to modify a DEERS record. You need a special access card, "You have to be authorized. You need a background check and a password."

THE LAST VOYAGE OF THE USS VREELAND

"Vreeland's an extremely intelligent man," recalls Assistant District Attorney for McComb County Eric Kaiser. "He weaves truth and fiction so well, it's difficult to sort out."

Vreeland's own website proudly displays a photograph of the USS Vreeland on the home page, a battleship named for Charles E. Vreeland, one of the first directors of ONI. Delmart has claimed on his website and in interviews to be the great-grandson of this Charles E. Vreeland. However, a couple of days' research into Vreeland's heredity shows that his great-grandfather is actually Charles R. Vreeland, a railroad worker.

Vreeland's half-brother Terry Weems, a country-western guitarist who lives in Alabama, has given numerous interviews and popped up on various websites to discuss his brother. Weems seems to possess a feud-level obsession to discredit Vreeland's connections to intelligence. "He shoves out a lot of B.S. and people like you swallow it down like your favorite drink," he wrote.

During Vreeland's early Naval career, Weems remembers, he watched his half-brother, "yelling at an admiral over the phone and being AWOL. He was arrested in the credit union. I was there also for that. He was on crack really bad during that time."

Weems also claims that Vreeland stole and illegally used his Social Security Number, but was unable to provide proof. In an interview on Toronto radio station CKLN, Weems said Delmart is the "luckiest criminal I've ever known...He's very good at identity theft, and, after a lot of them years, he was probably wanted, but he was able to elude police using a fake ID."

Vreeland reportedly scammed a furniture store in Michigan of forty thousand dollars worth of goods using an American Express card that AmEx later claimed wasn't properly authorized. The merchant got stuck holding the bag.

There's something askew with that AmEx bill. Vreeland's official criminal records say he wasn't there. While he was ripping off the Scott Shuptrine Furniture store on December 21, 1999, he was simultaneously in New York, where he was arrested for Grand Larceny Auto. Vreeland claims he was in jail in New York City around this time from a drunk driving incident on December 17. He also says that his friend, Josh Emley, was approved to use his AmEx card in Michigan.

In interviews, the only conviction Vreeland will admit to

deserving is the December 17, 1999 drunk driving arrest, the one in New York. As detailed in his Canadian affidavit, he had been at a party at the United Nations with military friends from Naval Intelligence. After some serious boozing, Vreeland drove a limo the wrong way through Times Square and collided with another car. Since an arrest record would probably list all the passengers, the arrest, bail, and court records of the incident could help substantiate Vreeland's alleged Navy connections, if these records still exist.

Searches at the New York City Office of Court Administration, as well as the Clerk's office at the New York Criminal Court, came up with zero records of an arrest, a pending prosecution, or a conviction in NYC, at any time. The searches used all five of Vreeland's aliases and each came up empty. Vreeland says that he was released December 21, 1999, "at the Navy's request. They got me out of there quick."

Speaking of quick exits, a search of Vreeland's arrest records in South Bend, Indiana is also insightful: on February 7, 2000, Vreeland violently resisted arrest, after being suspected of stealing a red Porsche. As the Mishawaka Police Department records show, he was charged with burglary and battery to a police officer after he punched and kicked an Officer Kasznia. Yet, the case ended abruptly. The police report ends with, "the suspect ... released without any identification."

ONI AND CIA

Al Martin, a Vietnam veteran and author, is a former member of the ONI. He believes that Vreeland is also ONI. Martin's memoir of the Iran Contra scandal, *The Conspirators*, is based on his five years in Latin America. He describes ONI as possessing "a mechanism before the CIA even existed. They had contacts in foreign intelligence services and in foreign governments that the CIA never could have hoped to obtain...The CIA can't control any of its own assets domestically because it's against the law for it to do so, thus the ONI is obviously in a superior position. ONI is where the real deep control is. It's where the real deep secrets are kept."

According to *A Tangled Web: A History of CIA Complicity in Drug International Trafficking,* an independent report read into the Congressional Record in 1998 by Rep. John Conyers (D-Mich.), the ONI has been dealing with criminals and shady characters since the end of World War II. ONI worked with the U.S. Italian Mafia, including S. C. Luciana, a.k.a. Lucky Luciano, to fight communism in Italy, gather intelligence for the Allied Invasion of Sicily, and control the ports in the U.S. during wartime. After Luciano was pardoned from jail for his work with ONI (and CIA precursor, the Office of Strategic Services), he went back to Italy and became a kingpin in the heroin trade. Around this time, ONI also worked with Chinese mafia to take control of the opiate trade, helping to form the "Golden Triangle" which traded heroin and various forms of currency and contraband between Thailand/Burma, Laos/Vietnam, and China's Yunnan Province.

In Al Martin's experience with the Iran/Contra operation "Black Eagle," crooks and highly intelligent con men were always part of the team. "Black Eagle" was "narcotics trafficking, massive fraud, and weapons deals" with con man extraordinaire Lawrence Hamil at the center. Martin remembers, "Hamil [was] not just a simple con man, a government-connected swindler and money launderer, as people seem to think. He was very deeply involved in all sorts of political deals at the same time."[55]

THE JUNKYARD DOG

"There were certain things in the note...clues to get people to contact others to contact me." Vreeland says, as he orders a double Bacardi and Coke.

"I mean, like the reference to the 'M-234 RAGS.' Those weapons were sold to Malaysia. I wrote that to get Eva Teleki to contact me. She had been involved in the sale. She contacted Leo Wanta and said, 'This guy needs our help.'"

Wanta is a former U.S. Department of Treasury operative and former Somali Ambassador to Switzerland, among other things. The M-234 Ring Airfoil Grenade is an attachment for an M-16 machine gun that creates an anti-riot, crowd-control stun effect. I contacted Teleki, who denied selling anything to Malaysia. But she did speak highly of Vreeland, confirming that he is a former officer of the ONI. Both Teleki and Vreeland have formal business relationships with Leo Wanta.

On February 13, 2002, a former U.S. Attorney named Tom Henry wrote Vreeland a letter. Henry, who is Leo Wanta's legal advisor, put Vreeland through a series of tests attempting to see

55 http://www.almartinraw.com /uri1.html

if he could recognize certain "passwords or security code names." Vreeland aced it. Henry's letter concluded, "On best information and belief I am of the opinion that my clients would endorse that you gathered the information that you have shared with my client while acting in the capacity of an 'intel op' agent of the U.S. Government." In the past, Henry has worked with the Department of Justice in the Ford Administration before moving on to become a consultant on business matters in China.

Wanta describes himself as Ronald Reagan's former "taskmaster" and has an extensive resumé of his own. It includes work for the CIA, Department of Treasury, and the NSC, as well as deals involving foreign currencies, arms, and precious metals. Wanta worked on the 1988 Bush Presidential campaign. His collected correspondence includes notes from George Herbert Walker Bush, the Nixon White House, and various senators. After the Soviet withdrawal from Afghanistan, it was Wanta who was sent in to repossess Stinger anti-aircraft missiles from the Mujahedeen. According to Claire Sterling's book *Thieves' World*, Wanta was the central figure in an operation to destabilize the Russian Ruble with White House approval in the late '80s/early '90s. The attack on the currency hastened the crumbling of the Soviet Union. In our original April interview, Vreeland quipped, "I know people who know George Bush Sr. personally." He was talking about Wanta. Tom Hanneghan, a powerful Los Angeles Democrat and commodities trader speaks of Wanta with both criticism and credibility, "He worked for the U.S. intelligence agencies. He helped bring down the Soviet communist government. He's a brilliant engineer, lots of technical skills. He did a great job. He probably gathered too much knowledge for his own sake."

Ambassador Leo E. Wanta

Wanta told me he was Ronald Reagan's favorite "junkyard dog." He remembers, "Reagan had no faith in DC politicians, he liked his 'junkyard dogs.'" According to Wanta, Reagan praised him for his ability to get special tasks executed quickly, without going through normal channels.

In 1988, Wanta was in the news for trying to sell thirty thousand automatic pistols to Manuel Noriega. Wanta explained to me that this was a part of a scheme to enable the U.S. to identify every member of the Panamanian military. Shortly thereafter, on December 20, 1989,[56] Bush invaded Panama, swiftly arrested Noriega, put a pro-U.S. regime in control of the Panama Canal, and left an estimated three thousand civilians dead.

56 George Gedda, Associated Press, April 9, 1988: "Proposed Gun Deal Exposed by Panamanian Officer," First lines: "A rebel member of Panama's Defense Forces has smuggled out a memo detailing the efforts of military strongman Manuel Antonio Noriega to buy thousands of pistols from an American arms dealer. The memo, marked 'urgent' and 'confidential,' was sent to Noriega on April 1 by Leo Wanta, president of AmeriChina Global Management Group Inc., an arms exporting firm based in Appleton, Wis."

Wanta's net worth in 1992 was $432 billion, according to tax documents prepared in anticipation of Wanta's plans to move back to the U.S., pay federal income taxes from offshore business deals, and retire. This $432 billion was not exactly all cash, according to Wanta—a lot of it was tied up in "prime bank guarantees," a kind of certified deposit that Wanta would purchase from top "credit-worthy" banks and trade at a profit, on behalf of the U.S. Treasury Department. Under the aegis of Aneko Credit PTE, LTD, in Singapore, Wanta engaged in a complex form of private banking, comparable to arbitrage but cash-based, high-speed, and highly volatile. Wanta accumulated $22 million each day that a prime bank guarantee was purchased at a par value of $100 million. When Wanta wanted to retire, it was not to be. In early June of 1993, Leo Wanta was appointed the Somali ambassador to Canada and Switzerland, in what he says was an effort to help make Somalia a safe launching ground for the U.S. military. According to reports from Wanta, Henry, and Vreeland, Wanta traveled to Switzerland with notorious financier Marc Rich between June 30 and July 3, 1993. According to Wanta, during their trip to Switzerland, Wanta helped to negotiate the financing for "UN Contract 4," a back channel deal that he claims worked with various sources of international capital to funnel funds to buy peace in the Middle East. Each side of the Rabin/PLO Agreement would get $5 billion. (Although UN Contract 4 was not ratified, it was a precursor to the Oslo Peace Accord that was signed in a dramatic White House ceremony in September, 1993.) According to Wanta, the Clinton White House, acting through attorney Vince Foster, asked that $250 million be placed into the Swiss account of the Children's Defense Fund as a charitable byproduct of the deal.

When Marc Rich received a controversial pardon from President Clinton, it was widely reported that Rich had worked as a spy for Israel. Articles in the *LA Times* and the *New York Post* cited evidence from the House Oversight Committee that claimed Rich performed numerous secret missions for the Israeli government, including helping secure back-channel financing for an Israeli-Palestinian peace deal. Wanta remembers that Rich was also looking out for number one. "Marc Rich was doing a tremendous amount of things against what we were doing in Russia and Switzerland. He was doing deals with Iraqis, Iranians, Swiss banks." In 2001, Marc Rich was living in exile in Switzerland, facing American charges for racketeering, wire fraud, illegally selling oil to the Iranians, and owing $48 million in back taxes. On January 20, 2001, hours before he would leave office, Clinton pardoned him. Israel's then-Prime Minister Ehud Barak had called Clinton the night before asking for the pardon and stating it was "important...financially."[57]

Back in 1993, in Switzerland, Wanta says he had orders to arrest Rich, and, if that failed, to assassinate him. According to the story from both Vreeland and Wanta, the ONI had snipers nearby when Wanta and Rich were on a ferry to a casino in France, traveling across Lake Geneva from Lausanne. The sniper from ONI couldn't get a clear shot off, and was told to stand down. According to their story, that sniper was Delmart Vreeland.[58]

Something went awry after Switzerland. Three weeks later, Vince Foster was found dead in Fort Marcy Park, just outside DC in Arlington, VA. The death was swiftly ruled a suicide by the park police, despite their paltry experience with suicide investigations. (And as I'll point out below, the anomalies in Foster's death were glossed over by future 9/11 Commissioner Richard Ben-Veniste, and future Director of Homeland Security Michael Chertoff.)

The day prior to the discovery of Vince Foster's body, FBI director William Sessions was fired. His temporary replacement, Floyd Clarke, let the bumbling park police run the non-investigation of Foster's death, despite the victim being the First Lady's best friend and confidante. Sessions later stated outright that Clarke believes he was fired to hamper a Foster death investigation. Three independent criminal evidence experts hired by *Strategic Investor* newsletter studied the Foster suicide note and declared it a forgery.

Wanta was arrested by Swiss authorities and deported on the flimsy pretext of State of Wisconsin tax evasion charges. Wanta was extradited without a warrant and flown from Switzerland in leg, arm, and neck shackles. The Wisconsin prosecutor levied tax evasion charges for 1989 through 1991, although Wanta had not lived in the U.S. since 1985. He was convicted and imprisoned after a swift trial, despite the fact that the IRS stated he did not owe any federal taxes from the same period.

When Wanta's case came before Wisconsin court in Madison, there was outright ridicule of him in the media. Dennis Ullman, the lead tax collection agent for Wisconsin on the case, was friendly with Cliff Miller of the *Appleton Post*, according to sources close to the Wanta case. Miller stories treated Wanta like a lunatic with delusions of a glorious past. But any journalist with a Lexis/Nexis account could see that Wanta

57 See the Clinton/Barak Transcript of a conversation right before the pardon, at
http://www.cnn.com/2001/ALLPOLTICS/08/20/rich.pardon /index.html
58 At the time, Vreeland wanted the Marc Rich sniper job off the record. But Leo Wanta was happy to talk about it on record. It seemed fishy—I decided to call Vreeland up and "ambush" him with a set of technical questions about precision riflery. I asked "What shoulder weapon were you using in the Wanta situation?"/"Winchester" /What caliber was it? /"370" /What scope make and magnification? /"Starlight." /Mag? / "Yes" /Lens? /"6x6" /What rounds did you use? /"Basic copper tops, 280 grain. /Was it a hot load or a sub sonic load? /"Hot." Vreeland stated that his firing accuracy is 98 percent. An expert on snipers confirmed that Vreeland knew his guns.

actually was the "global businessman" he claimed to be. The older news clip about Noriega and the arms deal were all part of the public record. But in 1993, consistent jabs in the Madison newspapers destroyed Wanta in the court of public opinion. Wanta was not allowed to hire his own attorney, and his court-appointed one, John Chavez, didn't believe his story. Leo Wanta's sanity was often questioned in court, but he was never found incompetent to stand trial. Wanta's international friends relate that the experience took its toll on him, both mentally and physically.

Right before his trial, Wanta was denounced as a "snake oil salesman" and an "egregious thief" in *Thieves World* by Claire Sterling. The problem is, the late Claire Sterling was closely connected to the CIA, according to multiple sources. Sounds like the ambassador pissed off somebody at the top. Maybe it has something to do with the two thousand tons of Soviet gold he was attempting to move on international markets, right after the fall of the U.S.S.R.

Today, Ambassador Wanta remains under house arrest in Wisconsin. Wanta claims that when he was arrested, he was forced to leave behind about $200 billion in prime bank guarantees. "Lawfully earned funds," Wanta says, that international banks and governments have been allowed to "use free of charge" since he's been detained (when you total up the interest and the capital that can accumulate through smart use of $200 billion, Wanta says, it comes out to about $27.6 trillion). After Wanta and his counsel, Henry, confirmed to their satisfaction that Vreeland was in fact an intelligence operative, they hired Delmart Vreeland to help recover some of the money.

In a late night, three-way conversation between us, Vreeland recently blurted out to Wanta, "Who has controlled me in the last eight months?"

Wanta gruffly stated, "ONI."

"Where would they get orders from?"

"Cheney."

If that's true it might help explain why the vice president has never rescinded his claim that Iraq was involved in 9/11. Maybe he got it straight from Delmart Vreeland. Or vice versa.

Admonished later by Vreeland for saying too much about Switzerland, Leo Wanta replied, "I'm in constant pain; rheumatism, arthritis, I have not received proper medical care. I'm not afraid anymore."

Mike Ruppert was also present at this radio interview, and added some big picture analysis: "None of us are saints, but all of us have moments in which we try to do the right thing, and that's when we need to be supported. This is not over yet."

On August 13, 2002, a death certificate with Vreeland's name and details on it showed up on the web. Apparently, he shot himself in the back of the head. The Internet was abuzz with the rumor. I called the dead man. He was unfazed, "We used to do this all the time. It's a way to let someone know they are after you."

Vreeland had an extradition hearing on Monday, September 9, 2002, but he didn't show. He had spent the entire day before with his attorney, Paul Slansky, who later told the *Toronto Sun* that Vreeland had been concerned that certain forces "were going to shut him up and do something to him."

The next day, a bench warrant was issued for his arrest. That night, Slansky entered Vreeland's apartment with the police. It looked like a cyclone had hit it. It was ransacked, but without signs of bloodshed. If Vreeland had left town of his own free will, it didn't show. Slansky stated, "Everything is there, his toothbrush, his underwear, his shaving gear, everything."

His attorneys speculated that Vreeland had been killed. However, on Wednesday, October 20, 2004, Delmart Vreeland was arrested in Hampton, Iowa. Police traced him when he used a gas station credit card linked to his name. Vreeland was extradited back to Colorado, where, using the identity of "Clayton Steeves" he had skipped out on child prostitution charges two weeks earlier. As of this writing, he's in Colorado, awaiting trial. Seven months after extradition, he was still being kept in the local county jail.

I tried to get documentation on Vreeland's case but I ran into a firewall. Douglas County officials refused because the case was "an open investigation."

Vreeland then called me on Saturday night, June 11, 2005— our first conversation since 2002. For some reason, he couldn't talk about certain things, or people like Ambassador Wanta. I asked about the child sex charges and he gave me a Federal case number for a case that hadn't been sealed yet. In those Federal District Court documents Vreeland made reference to a "Federal Non-Disclosure Agreement" he had signed with the U.S. Government. "The USG is not attacking me nor helping me, that is the agreement."

Vreeland said he had seen the film, "Conspiracy of Silence," and he indicated that speculation about his past along those lines was fair game. When I asked directly about the pedophilia charges, Vreeland implied that the charges were false because they came from someone with "twenty-seven arrests" on their record. Not exactly a straight answer. In fact, submission of extraneous information tends to indicate discomfort with a question, in the parlance of professional lie-detectors. In the documents Vreeland submitted to court, he no longer made reference to Joey as his "son" but as his "roommate" or "adopted son." Thanks to a legal maneuver from Tom Henry, Joey, a Canadian citizen, was deported back to Canada.

According to his Federal District Court complaint, Vreeland "has been in maximum security since October 20, 2004—denied counsel, medical treatment, due process, bail, witnesses and physical evidence has been lost...." Vreeland has thirty-eight cents in his prison account.

Reading his 178-page court file was like returning to the abyss: the handwritten, amateur legalese, the passionate arcane excuses. But one thing jumps out—Vreeland tells the court the entire story about his 9/11 note, spying in Moscow, etc. The story hadn't changed. The details were identical to the story he told four years earlier. There was even more information there, now that Vreeland himself was writing it.

The question now becomes: who is listening?

The Big Wedding:

CHAPTER 6

A NATIONAL DISGRACE: THE 9/11 COMMISSION REPORT

The 9/11 Commission Report pays lip service to the value of the "investigative journalists and watchdog organizations." But the Commission refused to call any 9/11 watchdogs or investigative journalists to testify. Anyone who attended the hearings could see they instead brought in fellow bureaucrats, politicians, spies, and policy wonks. They listened to a parade of mind-blowingly dull chatter. In the report, when their witnesses repeatedly "don't recall" the answers, the Commission accepts that at face value. "Our aim has not been to assign blame," the Commission admits in the preface. They trumpet not assigning blame as if it's a virtue. Perhaps the inability to come to conclusions is a plus in an age of secrecy, subjectivism, and intransigent bureaucracy.

The 9/11 Commission Report is published by the employee-owned, independent press W. W. Norton & Co. The writing style goes out of its way to appear informal. It's so hip that it makes occasional references to movies like "Wag the Dog," and will occasionally float some vague rhetoric about the importance of civil liberties. The report seems to be going out of its way to not look like what it is: government propaganda.

The law that created the "9/11 Commission" demands that the Commission "not have personal (or other) ties to senior Bush officials or senior officers in key government agencies, which are being investigated by the Commission." Yet half of the members worked directly for the Bush and Clinton White Houses. In mid-January, two Commissioners, Jamie Gorelick and Philip Zelikow, testified about their own past involvement in creating terrorism policy. "Members of the Commission" are not supposed to have "links of any kind, business or otherwise, to the alleged perpetrators or 'financiers' of 9/11, including the bin Laden family." But six Commission members are DC lawyers, and the firms they represent aren't exactly pro-bono public defenders.

LET'S MEET OUR PANEL:

Philip Zelikow, Executive Director of the Commission, is a former National Security Council member who has co-written articles with ex-CIA Director John Deutch. Zelikow and Condoleezza Rice co-wrote a book on the glories of a unified Germany in 1997. Zelikow got to know Rice so well he mooned over her to the *Washington Post*, "She can walk into a gathering of almost any kind and instantly find a poised way of handling herself, whether in a one-on-one meeting with a Russian marshal or a church group in Palo Alto or a corporate group." Zelikow is a member of the International Institute for Strategic Studies, a London-based diplomacy think tank often associated with British intelligence.

Thomas Kean, Chairman of the Commission, is a former governor of New Jersey. Kean also happens to be a director for the oil giant Amerada Hess, which at the time of the hearings was in the middle of the "Hess-Delta" joint venture with Delta Oil of Saudi Arabia. Delta Oil is owned by Khalid bin Mahfouz, formerly of BCCI. Kean is on the Board at the National Endowment on Democracy, an institution that doles out millions of dollars to groups that fight labor-unions. During the Iran/Contra hearings, the White House claimed that NED "ran Project Democracy," Oliver North's operation in Nicaragua.[59]

Lee Hamilton, Commission Vice-Chair, was chairman of the House Select Committee on Iran/Contra. He told "Frontline" that he didn't indict Reagan or Bush because he didn't think it would be "good for the country." Hamilton, while chairman, caved in to political pressure from a hawkish, fellow-congressman from Wyoming by the name of Dick Cheney. Earlier, with his Congressional Task Force in 1992, Lee Hamilton exonerated President George H.W. Bush of any involvement in the "October Surprise" scandal, despite strong evidence from former White House aide Gary Sick, and Israeli and Russian intelligence.

The Big Wedding:

John Lehman is a protégé of Henry Kissinger. While Secretary of the Navy, he covered up an inquiry into a U.S. Navy pedophilia ring in Coos Bay, Oregon in 1982. Independent journalist Wayne Madsen first reported this. He would know, he was serving there at the time. Lehman is the author of *On Seas of Glory: Heroic Men, Great Ships, and Epic Battles of the American Navy.*

Bob Kerrey: In 2001, reports emerged that then-Lieutenant Kerrey led a mission that slaughtered thirteen civilians in Vietnam. Although a progressive Democrat, Kerrey has worked with right-wing advocacy group Project for a New American Century as a member of the Committee for the Liberation of Iraq. Kerrey as Nebraska Governor was instrumental in the cover-up of the 1989 Bush White House callboys scandal, as documented in *The Franklin Cover-Up* and in the documentary "Conspiracy of Silence."

Richard Ben-Veniste came to prominence in Washington as chief of the Watergate Task Force, and was later President Clinton's Senate-appointed lawyer in the Whitewater investigation. But today, Ben-Veniste has direct connections to murky underworld figures. During Whitewater, Richard Ben-Veniste was the Senate-appointed defender of Clinton. In a widely criticized move, he then worked as a private attorney to defend Clinton friend and financier Truman Arnold from the same Whitewater investigation. In a similar fashion, Ben-Veniste earlier defended Barry Seal, the shady, low-level Iran/Contra figure who flew cocaine exports from the Contras into Mena, Arkansas. According to letters among Barry Seal's papers, his lawyer, Ben-Veniste, at one point was eager to get back his "two briefcases of legal materials which you have been holding, as soon as possible."[60] Was Seal blackmailing his own lawyer? Perhaps we'll never know, as Seal died a gruesome death on the streets of Baton-Rouge, machine-gunned in his car at a stoplight, assassinated "Medellin-cartel style."

Jamie Gorelick, the only female member of the panel, is ironically the closest to that network of good ol' Ivy-leaguers, the CIA. She is a member of the CIA's National Security Advisory Panel. Gorelick was a Pentagon lawyer until 1993, when she was appointed Deputy Attorney General of the U.S. Shortly after Gorelick was handed a post on the Commission, she joined the Washington law firm of Wilmer, Cutler & Pickering, in July 2003. Just months earlier, that firm had announced that it would defend Saudi Prince Mohammed al Faisal, the third in command in the Saudi government. Al Faisal is a defendant in

59 *Washington Post,* February 16, 1987; also see *New York Times,* February 15, 1987
60 Daniel Hopsicker, *Barry and The Boys* (Eugene, OR: Mad Cow Press, 2001)

the billion-dollar lawsuits brought on by the families of the victims of 9/11.

James R. Thompson is chairman of the Chicago law firm of Winston & Strawn, which has defended both tobacco giant Philip Morris and the food genetics-modifier Monsanto against plaintiffs in class action lawsuits.

Slade Gorton is a former Republican senator from Washington State. Gorton served on the Presidential Consumer Advisory Board under Ford and Carter from '75-'77. He is now a lawyer in the Seattle firm of Preston, Gates and Ellis. Among their clients: Delta Air Lines and Boeing Employees' Credit Union.

Fred F. Fielding has worked as White House Counsel to Nixon and Reagan. He was there during the Watergate cover-up when his boss, John Dean, confided that he was considering destroying evidence. Fielding didn't exactly object. Fielding claims no knowledge of Iran/Contra, because he "left the White House in 1986." But that's suspicious. Evidence shows that Reagan and Bush authorized arms shipments to Iran in 1985, and earlier. As recently as 2001, Fielding worked for the White House as clearance counsel during the Bush-Cheney presidential transition.

Timothy J. Roemer is the clean one. Sort of. Well certainly he's the young one. He's the only Commissioner who helped create the Commission, when he was a Congressman in the House. From 1991-2003, Roemer was a Democratic Representative from Indiana, where he served on the Permanent Select Committee on Intelligence, and passed legislation on welfare reform and progressive issues. He served on the bipartisan Joint Inquiry, which was critical of U.S. intelligence failures. Of course, the Joint Inquiry felt it proper to keep its harshest criticisms of the White House in a classified section of their report. Thanks, Tim.

A KOOKY THEORY

In May 2004, after observing Commission hearings at the New School in New York City, I was personally disgusted by the joking and the fun that the Commission members seemed to be having. I walked to the subway in the rain. My naïveté was gone. I realized that this Commission had access to the truth, but they were deliberately ignoring it. They wasted $14 million dollars of our tax money.

In July 2004, they published a pack of lies. The *Report* may be the most literary work ever authored by a group of ten. "Tuesday, September 11, 2001, dawned temperate and nearly cloudless in the eastern United States" is the opener. It's that undergraduate formula: Start with the weather. The *Report* then moves on to tell a selective conspiracy theory.

The ten DC insiders that make up the Commission did their best not to look at any of the strange anomalies that surround 9/11. On page 20, for example, the Commission reports that an air defense controller at the Northeast Air Defense Sector (NEADS) reacted to the hijackings by asking, "Is this real-world, or exercise?" The terrorists somehow knew to strike on the morning that NORAD, NEADS, and the Joint Chiefs of Staff were preoccupied with three different air defense drills (operations named things like "Vigilant Guardian," etc.). Although victim family member Mindy Kleinberg brought up this coincidence on the first day of hearings, the Commission only mentions Vigilant Guardian as an afterthought, buried in the notes section in tiny type in the back of the book.

Regarding the background of Osama bin Laden, the Commission boldly dives head-on into the history of the terrorist ringleader's training as a Mujahedeen by the CIA: *they deny it.*

As we've already established, bin Laden was the CIA's point man in Afghanistan in the '80s; through Pakistan. And the 9/11 Commission shows its cards by trying to repeat the CIA's public claim that bin Laden had "no relationship whatsoever" to the Agency: they soften it a little with "bin Laden received little or no assistance from the United States" in Afghanistan. The Commission denies that members of the bin Laden family were flown out of the U.S. on September 13, before airspace was open.

Before they published *The 9/11 Commission Report*, there was something benign about pointing out the possible conflicts of interest inside the Commission. Reporting on the amusing proximity of Commissioners to present government and intelligence organizations felt like a salacious digging of dirt. But now that the *Report* is out, it's a best seller. In publishing circles, in 2004, there was loose talk about it being nominated for a National Book Award. In print, the conflicts of interest are no longer tolerable. Now that we see what the conflicts produced, the lies of omission here are criminal. *They amount to the willful ignorance of the cause of homicide of 2,986 people.*

The *Report* publishes an edited version of the famous August 6, 2001 Presidential Daily Brief. Here we learn the "FBI is conducting approximately seventy full field investigations throughout the U.S. that it considers bin Laden-related." Really? Seventy different investigations? Then let's hear about them. The *Report* won't go there. The *Report* doesn't comment on how "seventy different investigations" contrasts with the earlier FBI claim that the terrorists pulled off 9/11 with "no outside help" from U.S.-based organizations.[61] The *Report* won't go anywhere near the issue of the FBI whistle-blowers who tried to investigate bin Laden-related terrorists, but were smacked down. On page 247, we meet Minneapolis terrorist-to-be Zacarias Moussaoui, but not *Time* "Person of the Year" Coleen Rowley, the FBI whistle-blower who couldn't get a FISA warrant from headquarters on him.

Terrorist financing is covered with a guileless "we don't know exactly where the money came from" manner. There is no mention of FBI Special Agent Robert Wright, who tracked down and seized $1.4 million of bin Laden-related funds before 9/11. His higher-ups fought him every step of the way. After the carnage of 9/11, Wright understandably broke down and, through tears, apologized on C-SPAN to 9/11 victims' families. "The FBI...allowed 9/11 to happen," he told the world. "FBI management intentionally and repeatedly thwarted and obstructed my investigations into Middle Eastern terrorist financing."

Both Rowley and Wright point to the FBI's David Frasca, the FBI's Radical Fundamentalist unit chief. Despite multiple denunciations, Frasca was promoted to number three in charge of Domestic Terrorism. Frasca is not mentioned in the Report.

The Commission can't ignore the Saudi/Pakistan/CIA menage-à-trois that has been going on since BCCI and the Afghan civil war. It's just that the most interesting details on this have been reported by the international press, and, as a rule, the Commission ignores stories not picked up by the lapdog U.S. media. So, the fact that Pakistani ISI director General Ahmad wired $100 thousand to Mohamed Atta on September 10 is not covered. *The Times of India* and *Agence France-Presse* reported it, and General Ahmad was forced to step down because of it. But stateside, these facts languish unused. Instead, it's pointed out that General Ahmad happened to be in DC, meeting with Representative Porter Goss and Senator Bob Graham on the morning of 9/11. The Commission does cover how Deputy Secretary of State Dick Armitage used this to force Pakistan to help with the invasion of Afghanistan.

The Big Wedding:

To their credit, the subjects that the Commission does cover are well-researched. Al Qaeda is the result of a combination of historical factors; terrorism itself has changed. The global poor used to hijack planes to call for the release of prisoners. Now, in increasingly desperate times, terrorists have crossed over into direct martyrdom. The Commission coolly observes this, but doesn't examine why globalization has created such increased desperation.

The toughest critics of the Commission, the "9/11 Truth Movement," believe that 9/11 must have been the product of a military stand-down. Earlier in 2001, sixty-seven jets going off course were handled by established protocols, so why couldn't fighter jets be scrambled on 9/11? The *Report* points out the crucial difference that morning: the terrorist pilots turned their transponders off, thus making the planes more difficult to locate. But wait: wasn't NORAD trained to counter an attack by Soviet MiGs? MiGs, presumably, wouldn't be flying with transponders, either.

The *Report* amuses itself with little anecdotes. They claim that power struggles and bureaucratic red tape prevented the U.S. from seizing or killing bin Laden before 9/11. The CIA wanted to borrow the Predator spy plane from the Air Force to spy on the mastermind, but didn't want to have to pay for it if they crashed it.

The Commission often mentions the love life of terrorist Ziad Al-Jarrah and his European girlfriend, Aysel Senguen, with whom he often visited. It's a heart-breaking story, especially their last visit. But at a certain point, you wonder if it's just in there to fill space.

The narcotics trafficking of U.S. allies, intelligence operatives, and international assets is a dirty subject. Too weird for the U.S. media, it's strictly the realm of Internet researchers, bitter government critics, lefty academic historians and ... the 9/11 Commission. The report deserves credit for effectively admitting, late in its findings, that with its newly installed leader, Harmid Karzai, Afghanistan is exporting an embarrassing amount of heroin. The *Report* neither condemns nor approves, it just stoically observes, with a CIA-level cool, "the United States...has largely avoided confronting the...problem of narco-trafficking." Thanks.

Among the Commission's stellar recommendations are: "routinizing, even bureaucratizing, the exercise of imagination." Or how about: "Recommendation: ...attack terrorists and their organizations." Yes, Master! I especially like the throwaway

61 Amy Goldstein, "Hijackers Led Core Group," *Washington Post,* September 30 , 2001; Goldstein's piece parrots the FBI "no outside help" statement with little analysis on the contradictions here. In return, Goldstein won the Pulitzer in 2002.

cocktail party generalization of "every major religion will spawn violent zealots." This stuff is like a small press conspiracy theory written without an editor! Wait, this IS a conspiracy theory! It's a kooky theory that terrorists with box cutters were able to defeat a $400 billion-a-year war machine. But it's way out there, man. It's interesting, sure, but the facts don't hold up.

At ten dollars retail, the *Report* could be the cheapest conspiracy theory on the market. It undercuts more rigorous, encyclopedic tomes like *Terror Timeline* by Paul Thompson. The *Report* is half-truths at half-price.

The Commission recommends that a passport be required to cross into Canada and Mexico. That recommendation will become phased into law in 2008. The Commission calls for a more centralized, powerful national intelligence apparatus. That recommendation was put into place all too eagerly with the creation of a National Intelligence Director. The Bush White House got their first choice approved for the position: Iran/Contra black operative John Negroponte[62].

The Commission calls for an oversight office to protect civil liberties. Funny, that one got ignored. There's a quick reference in the *Report* to J. Edgar Hoover's harassment and concentrated assault on the Reverend Martin Luther King, Jr. and other activist organizations. Perhaps if the Commission spent more time on this subject, they'd realize that an unbridled police state necessarily damages civil liberties, no matter what you say you believe. Talk is cheap.

The *Report* climaxes in a grand paean to war-without-end. The enemy is dehumanized and depoliticized. You can't "bargain" or "negotiate" with terrorists. There is "no common ground," they can "only be destroyed or isolated." In other words, don't ask yourself how your enemy was created, or what the enemy believes about its justification. Don't look at bin Laden's own statements about the U.S.'s backing of Israel, and don't consider the motivating effect when Arab youth in the poorest countries on Earth watch Palestinian houses bulldozed on Al Jazeera.

The Report's final line is "we look forward to a national debate on the merits of what we have recommended, and we will participate vigorously in that debate."

Ha. A debate is the last thing the Commission wants. This Commission cuts off media access to reporters who ask tough

---

62 From 1981 to 1985, Negroponte was ambassador to Honduras, at a time when the U.S.-backed Honduran military committed 185 death squad murders. According to a staff assistant, Negroponte suppressed the embassy's own 1982 report on human rights abuses. U.S. military funding to Honduras went from four to $77 million during his tenure. The Reagan White House used Honduras as a staging ground for the illegal arming of the Contra rebels. Jose Miguel Vivanco, director of Human Rights Watch/America, called Negroponte the "ostrich ambassador," for his willingness to look the other way, making military objectives a higher priority than human rights.

The Big Wedding:

questions. (As we see, from my personal experiences, in the next chapter.)

The 9/11 Commission Report has topped the Warren Report on President Kennedy's murder as the greatest cover-up of all time. They advance an official story that high-level personnel at the White House, FBI, CIA, and the Department of Justice were just caught off guard. If that's the case, those groups should have been indicted for a lack of watchfulness. But since no indictment or punishment has been coming from the government, we must look elsewhere. First-hand witness testimony keeps pointing to the conclusion that the White House and their intelligence advisors knew about 9/11, and let it happen. God willing, a day is coming when the parties responsible will be tried in a high court.

But today, the FBI, CIA, and Department of Justice only receive a thank you in the introduction of *The 9/11 Commission Report.*

CHAPTER 7

"WHACKJOB!"
MY LIFE WITH
RICHARD BEN-VENISTE &
KENNETH FEINBERG

In February 2004, I published a two-part-series feature article about 9/11 anomalies for the *Long Island Press*, a New York City area newsweekly. I covered independent researchers like Daniel Hopsicker as well as Ellen Mariani, a 9/11 widow who is suing President Bush. Ellen Mariani is a brassy, grandmotherly lady from New Hampshire, who lost her husband Louis when Mohammed Atta flew their plane into the North Tower of the World Trade Center. Covering her case gave me an opportunity to interview the September 11 Victims Compensation Fund "Special Master," Kenneth Feinberg.

What happened between Feinberg and me never saw print, due to space considerations. But at the time, I was very excited to report it. Ms. Mariani's lawsuit named Kenneth Feinberg as one of the defendants, alongside both George Bushes, John Ashcroft, etc. Feinberg was named because Mariani and Berg held evidence that he had acted over and above his responsibilities as a Fund administrator. Instead of just being a paymaster who meted out an average of $1.5 million to each surviving family member, Feinberg seemed determined to recruit all victims' families into the Fund, whether they wanted the money or not.[63]

Ellen Mariani was refusing the money because she didn't like the attendant clause that prevented a victim from further

---

63 According to the *New York Times*, by June of 2004 the government had paid out five thousand families a total of $7 billion: "In exchange for giving up their right to sue...relatives of dead victims were told that the average payment would be about $1.5 million, tax free, after deductions for life insurance and other possible benefits." David W. Chen, "After Weighing Cost of Lives, 9-11 Fund Completes Its Task," *New York Times*, June 15, 2004.

legal action: against the airlines or, say, against Ashcroft. She fired her first lawyer for trying to manipulate her into taking the fund money. She then hired Chicago attorney Don Nolan, who happened to be an acquaintance of Kenneth Feinberg. On February 8, 2002, Feinberg wrote a generic thank you letter to all attorneys who had volunteered to help administer funds. But in a handwritten postscript to his friend "Don," Kenneth Feinberg urged Don Nolan to bring the combative Mariani into the fund.

The letter would have been innocuous if it had been discarded. But shortly thereafter, Nolan urged Mariani to see a psychiatrist. Mariani retorted by suggesting that he see one. And then she fired Nolan.

Kenneth Feinberg's extralegal influence-peddling indicated there might be some truth to Mariani's legal claim that his role was to "ensure all '9/11' families joined the fund to prevent any questions of liability, gross or criminal negligence on the part of Defendant Bush and his administration for failing to act and prevent the '9/11' attacks."

But I couldn't just quote from the lawsuit in my story. I had to find out for myself.

In early December 2003, I got Feinberg on the phone. We started off our interview with some chatting about the percentage of victims' families who were accepting the fund. With a deadline approaching, Feinberg was gunning for 90 percent, his "magic minimum."

Curtailing the small talk, I asked Mr. Feinberg if he knew that he was being sued by Ellen Mariani through attorney Phil Berg. I told him that there were allegations that he had used "strong arm tactics and hostility" towards the widow. Feinberg indicated that he didn't know who Mariani was.

I elucidated: "The allegations have to do with what they feel was a broach of attorney/client privilege. They allege that you contacted her one-time attorney; she used to be represented by Don Nolan, of the Nolan Law Group in Chicago, and they allege that you sent a letter to Don Nolan, urging Ms. Mariani to get into the fund. Do you know anything about that letter?"

Feinberg's answer? "Uhhhhhh. Nooo."

Then, a pause.

It could perhaps be interpreted as a contemplative moment, a quick mental strategizing session, or a debate with himself as to whether to lie to a reporter. And then, the lie.

We went off the record for a second, and when we got back on, things went like this:

The Big Wedding:

Hicks: So, you're saying that you don't have any knowledge of the letter.

Feinberg: I'm not saying that. On the record, here's what I'm saying. I have not seen this lawsuit, or read the complaint, so I cannot comment. I know nothing about it. And therefore cannot respond. **Hicks:** Right, but before we went off the record, you just said something like you didn't know about this letter, like you weren't familiar...

Feinberg: I'm not familiar with the letter.

Hicks: So you don't recall sending a letter on the...

Feinberg: [a degree louder] I have no recollection...I'm telling you what I want to put on the record. All I'm saying on the record, ALL I'm saying on the record is, I haven't seen the complaint, I don't know about the allegations. I have no comment. Unquote.

Hicks: Right, but before we went on the record....

Feinberg: [quite a few degrees louder] DO WHAT YOU WANT THEN. DO YOU HEAR WHAT I'M TELLIN' YA? NOW IF YOU WANT TO SAY, "BEFORE I WENT ON, AFTER I WENT ON, I DON'T RECALL THE LETTER" that's up to you. Now I'm just telling you what I'm saying, on the record. And that's all I'm saying on the record.

Hicks: Right, right, right. OK, because the...[pause] well, they say they have copies of this letter.

Feinberg: [sigh] I haven't seen the complaint. I know nothing about the complaint, or the allegations. Therefore I cannot respond to anything that's in the complaint.

Hicks: I understand you haven't been served papers...what have your experiences been with Ellen Mariani?

Feinberg: I have no experiences with Ellen Mariani.

Hicks: Well, you never wrote a hand-written note on this letter to Don Nolan?

Feinberg: Now listen to me, I'll tell you one more time.

Hicks: There's no reason to become adversarial here.

Feinberg: Yes there is.

Hicks: I'm pursuing this to the utmost.

Feinberg: I understand that. You're a good reporter. I don't know anything about this lawsuit, or the complaint. So I don't recall. I have no knowledge.

Hicks: That's the Ronald Reagan...

Feinberg: Look, I gotta get off the phone. This is where I am. When I see the complaint, Sander, give me a call. Maybe I'll have a comment on it. When I read it and see what she says and check my notes and my records, I may be able to respond. Right now, all I can tell you right now—and you're a, you're a good reporter—I have nothing personal, but all I can tell you right now is I have no recollection of any of this, and I will have to read the complaint before I can respond.

Hicks: Good enough. Thanks.

In her suit, Mariani's accused Feinberg of, "questionable strong-arm tactics and hostility." My conversation with Feinberg seemed to provide those accusations with merit.

There are other accusations in the Mariani/Berg racketeering suit that almost seem over the top. They accuse Feinberg of diverting Red Cross funds that were earmarked for victims' families to displaced downtown renters and FEMA workers. But after meeting Feinberg on the phone, and having our candid exchange, what might once have seemed outlandish in the Mariani suit now seems more like it deserves a day in court. One thing's for certain: Special Master Feinberg wasn't hired for his soft touch, or his compassion for the grieving.

PALAST ON FEINBERG

Right after my *Long Island Press* article was on the streets, the news came in that former New York Governor Mario Cuomo was suing the investigative journalist Greg Palast. Greg was a hero of mine, and someone I had talked to during the *Fortunate Son* years, before he became a best-selling author for his muckraking collection, *The Best Democracy Money Can Buy.*

Cuomo was suing over a line in *Democracy* that he claimed had defamed him.

Palast was standing by his reporting. I thought that this would be a good follow-up story, so I phoned Greg up. He related how he'd run "one of the biggest investigations ever" into the "creepy slime ball directors of Long Island's Shoreham Nuclear Plant," who had "lied day in and day out about the costs and safety of that plant." His investigation led Judge Jack Weinstein to believe that this nuclear power plant had defrauded the public of gross sums. The Judge was about to sentence plant-owners LILCO to a $4.8 million fine, when a go-between for Governor Cuomo intervened on behalf of the Long Island power company.

That go-between was Kenneth Feinberg.

Small world? It gets smaller—Judge Jack Weinstein was the same judge who suppressed NY FBI corruption related to the 1993 World Trade Center bombing. Weinstein refused to admit evidence from mafia scion Greg Scarpa, Jr. that proved the FBI's Lindley DeVecchio was in cahoots with mafia capo Greg Scarpa, Sr. DeVecchio had also been FBI whistle-blower Richard Taus's criminal squad supervisor. Judge Jack Weinstein denied Taus's recent habeus corpus appeal.

MY LIFE WITH RICHARD BEN-VENISTE

My experiences with Mr. Feinberg were oddly similar to the passive/aggressive bullying I received from Mr. Richard Ben-Veniste, the DC power-lawyer, friend of the Clintons, and 9/11 Commissioner.

My first impression of Richard Ben-Veniste was quite good. In his opening remarks on the Commission's first day of hearings, he was critical of the White House. I liked his terse lambasting. He asked why the White House had to drag its heels in approving security clearances for the Commission. After the hearings, I went up to Ben-Veniste and introduced myself. I had begun to do a little work with "INN World Report," a weekly news show on Free Speech TV. After a handshake, a smile, and a quick pitch, he agreed to come on the show the next day.

What happened next showed the great potential of television. Cameras don't lie. A government spokesperson or a top-shelf attorney can say "no comment" to a print reporter, and that reporter is left with nothing. But, if you try that on television, it is impossible for the viewer to not notice the corporeal tension that comes with that phrase. In Ben-Veniste's case, he effectively said "no comment" on three different occasions over the course of our fifteen minutes or so on camera. The Ben-Veniste interview showed the potential for what could become a new form of combative journalism, once television is in the hands of the people.

To prepare, I pulled Daniel Hopsicker's book on CIA drug-runner Barry Seal, *Barry and the Boys*, off the shelf. With that book in hand, I reviewed Ben-Veniste's accomplishments: a star prosecutor of Watergate, who had worked alongside Hillary Clinton and fought successfully for the release of Nixon's White House tapes. But from that point forward in his Washington career, he accumulated friendships with the mega-powerful and left behind the prosecution of corruption. To cite a few examples, Ben-Veniste worked alongside Clark Clifford (later of BCCI) in defending House Speaker Jim Wright from accusations of bribery. The really juicy "secret history of America," (which Daniel Hopsicker dug up) was Richard Ben-Veniste's defense of CIA asset and cocaine-smuggling pilot Barry Seal. Seal had flown repeated trips from Honduras into Governor Clinton's Mena, Arkansas airfield during the Iran/Contra era. According to George Stephanopoulos's political memoir *All Too Human*, Clinton was so pro-Contra that Stephanopoulos wasn't sure he could work for him. Barry Seal and Mena, Arkansas continue to be one of the least-understood aspects of the Iran/Contra scandal, especially by progressives. Stephanopoulos himself dismissively referred to the Mena allegations as mere conspiracy theory. This is a case of a severe lack of class-consciousness from the liberal intelligentsia. Too many assume that Clinton was morally above funding an anti-socialist militia through international narcotics trafficking, gunrunning, and hostage trading with Iran. But the facts show otherwise. Clinton had long earlier decided that his class loyalties were to the wealthy elite. I packed *Barry and the Boys* into my satchel and jumped on the train to the studio.

In our small talk before we rolled the cameras, I told Mr. Ben-Veniste about *Fortunate Son*, and we talked a little about the publishing business in New York.

To avoid looking greasy on camera, I put some powder on and asked if he would like some. I explained, "Once those lights are on, the heat can really make you sweat."

"You can't make me sweat," he said with a grin.

Barry and the Boys was under my chair. *We'll see,* I thought.

Before we rolled, I explained that we would talk, and any mistakes could be edited out. Ben-Veniste requested that we send him a copy of the broadcast. I agreed.

Once we were rolling, I improvised an introduction, and welcomed him to the show. Things started slow, but eventually became enlightening. This is how the show was eventually broadcast:

> HICKS: Well, it's really quite an honor to have an actual member of the National Commission here on "INN Report." We've been following with interest the development of the National Commission. My first question that I wanted to talk to you about is how you view what seems to be a somewhat antagonistic relationship between the White House and people who question 9/11. I'm speaking specifically about the controversy about funding—you mentioned in your introductory remarks about the lack of security clearances for the Commission—and let's go back a couple of months ago. You remember that there was some talk in the media about how Tom Daschle had been called by Bush and Cheney, and somewhat threatened on the phone about not letting the Joint Inquiry in Congress look in too closely at 9/11. What are your thoughts?

> BEN-VENISTE: Well, our statute provides us with authority to conduct a very broad inquiry; basically, to provide an investigation of 9/11 that's thorough, complete, and will withstand the scrutiny of history. And I feel confident that we have the kind of people on our Commission and our staff who are capable of doing that. Now, I have no comment on what you mentioned earlier about the controversy.

It's clear that the Joint Inquiry, which did an astonishingly good job in the time they had, was not afforded all the information they sought. Our mandate expects that we will build on the Joint Inquiry's investigation and we will not be re-inventing the wheel. But we go to places which the Joint Inquiry was not permitted to explore. So that's one of the basic tenets of what we are doing.

Hicks: What are those areas that the Joint Inquiry that Congress was not allowed to explore?

Ben-Veniste: They made certain requests for interviews of members of the White House and the National Security Council, and they didn't get all the information that they sought.

In retrospect, my next question should have been to repeat my last. "No, but maybe you didn't understand me. I asked you what were the areas that the Joint Inquiry couldn't explore, and how do you really think you'll be any different?"

Hicks: I don't know if you are able to comment, but there has been a lot of talk about—not in mainstream media, but in independent media-about the relationship between the Bush family and the Saudis. Let's say, George Herbert Walker Bush's membership on the Board of Directors of the Carlyle Group. Or the fact that, in 1978, young W. Bush received money through James Bath; who, it turned out, was working for the Saudis...Salem bin Laden. Are you familiar with this information...?

Ben-Veniste: I don't have any comment on that.

Hicks: America has such a bad history with these kinds of special investigations. We have these major historical events that are then investigated. Former Governor Kean yesterday made reference to two precedents: the Warren Commission Report on the assassination of JFK and the Roberts Commission Report on the Pearl Harbor attack. And he admitted that the results of both those commissions were inadequate and did not satisfy the majority of the people. So, if you prefer not to talk about specifics of the Bush/bin Laden connection, then let's talk about the specifics of a broader historical inquiry. How can the National Commission on 9/11 be different from the Warren Report?

Ben-Veniste: I think the better analogy is the Roberts Commission, which was created, almost immediately, after the attack at Pearl Harbor. And the shortcomings of that Commission's report were documented. There were several subsequent inquiries. And it turned out that the Roberts Commission did not fully utilize the information available, and that it came to conclusions, which were, I think, quite shortsighted and, indeed, in some cases, scapegoated individuals.

Hicks: We saw a panel come before the Commission of five people who had firsthand injury experience in 9/11. And they told stories that were traumatic and emotional. But they emphasized that they had no anger, were not going to point fingers. But then we had victims' family members on the next panel. And these people were, I felt, like, had a whole different level of knowledge and inquiry and were asking some very hard questions about the lack of aviation response from the military on 9/11. And, you know, there are people out there who are asking hard questions. And I thought that was somewhat represented on Monday by the lunchtime press conference with 9/11 Citizens Watch. I wanted to ask you if you had reviewed any of the materials on them or have you seen any...

BEN-VENISTE: I was eating lunch at lunchtime. And we had, I think, twenty minutes. The family members represent a broad spectrum of personal reaction to the horrific losses that they have suffered. And they have been a constant source to us, not only of motivation, but they have provided very useful insights and information. And we are honored to work with them and to keep a very close relationship with the family members.

HICKS: What are some of the questions that the family members are asking that you feel are valid?

BEN-VENISTE: They are asking a number of questions about how it happened, that things which we had in place....

HICKS: Try to, like, off the top of your head, what were some emotional, knowledgeable, rational reactions that you had—like, "wow, that's a good question. That really bugs me, too."

BEN-VENISTE: Well, the forms that were filled out by the hijackers to get into this country, that were obviously inadequate. Those are actually State Department forms for visas, which provided inadequate information. The real issues that I think were highlighted in the hearings by family members who had many questions, which we will address. Hopefully, we will provide answers, at least by statements from those who were responsible at the time, for why our country could not connect the dots, did not operate as our system is designed to operate. And that will inform the suggestions that we make for making our system better.

HICKS: Let's go back for a second and talk about what you just said about the immigration forms of the terrorist hijackers, how there just seems to be a disconnect. How could these people—it was pointed out that a couple of these people were on the CIA's list of terrorists; they had attended the terrorism conference and yet they were allowed to be in country. There was a gentleman you may know of, named Daniel Hopsicker? He's a former producer of NBC, and he wrote a book called *Barry and the Boys*. You are mentioned in it. It's about a former client of yours who is now deceased, Mr. Barry Seal. Are you familiar with this book?

BEN-VENISTE: No, I haven't read the book, but I did represent Barry Seal, who was convicted. He thereafter, on his own, became a government informant. He worked against the Sandinistas and that certainly is not the subject of this....

HICKS: That's not the subject of....

BEN-VENISTE: We have quite a bit to do here in our Commission without going into all my private practice. I certainly wouldn't want this to be an infomercial for Richard Ben-Veniste as a private attorney.

No one ever suggested to Mr. Ben-Veniste that the show may become an infomercial for his private practice. Ben-Veniste's unwillingness to discuss his late client, Barry Seal, is more likely indicative of a desire to avoid discussing his defense of a CIA-connected, Iran/Contra drug runner. As we will see in the exciting conclusion of our program....

HICKS: Not at all. But the question was, Daniel Hopsicker is...

BEN-VENISTE: So, if you wouldn't mind staying on our subject...

HICKS: Not at all.

BEN-VENISTE: I'd appreciate it.

HICKS: He did this interesting research on the web that you can get about the flight school in Florida, about the—and the connections between CIA and Rudi Dekkers, the Dutch national, who ran that flight school. I'm wondering if the Commission plans to investigate that?

BEN-VENISTE: I think you are going right for the capillary, if I may say so.

HICKS: You mean "the jugular?"

BEN-VENISTE: No, I mean "the capillary."

HICKS: You mean the fine detail?

BEN-VENISTE: I mean the things that are, the detail that is certainly not central to us getting started here. So, we are in the inception stages. We are getting started. Our inquiry is on its way.

HICKS: These are part of the questions which the families are asking, Citizens Watch......

BEN-VENISTE: I don't think anybody asked any questions about Mr. Hopsicker, whoever he may be.

HICKS: No the question is really about Rudi Dekkers and about—he's a Dutch National. Mohamed Atta was at his flight school doing cocaine with his girlfriend. If Mohamed Atta is technically a fundamentalist Muslim, what is he doing cocaine and going to strip bars with Rudi Dekkers' girlfriend?

BEN-VENISTE: You know, that's a heck of a question.

HICKS: (Laughter) It sure is. Right. Well then we agree on that. Maybe then we'll just sort of wrap it up at this point if you'd rather. I know you have a plane to catch.

BEN-VENISTE: Right.

HICKS: And I appreciate you being on the program.

BEN-VENISTE: Sure thing.

HICKS: And thank you very much.

BEN-VENISTE: You're welcome.

HICKS: (to camera) Thank you, "INN Report" reporting.

The elevator ride down to the street was silent and tense. When I wanted to do a follow-up interview for the *Long Island Press,* Ben-Veniste of course never returned my phone calls or emails. But what had really been so bad about the interview? I didn't freak out and accuse him of being an accessory to the cover-up to the murder of 2,989 folks in downtown Manhattan, just because he used Oxford Debate Team tactics to deflect my questions. When he said the Huffman Aviation/Rudi Dekkers question was a "capillary" I didn't overturn the table and scream, "No, MAN, I'm actually jumping up and down on the NERVE of this whole situation—because if the CIA is connected to the flight school that trained three of the four of these guys, and the FBI is down there covering up the trail, I'd like to hear what exactly you guys are thinking of covering in your hearings?"

Au contraire, I was diplomatic. Effectively the answer I got was a tense acknowledgment that I had gone into protected territory. It's not what you say; it's how you say it. Ben-Veniste wasn't dismissive or informal with the capillary line. He was perfectly still. Straight. An electrically-charged security fence.

So, I couldn't get Mr. Ben-Veniste to comment on the new stuff I was discovering for the *Long Island Press.* But he clearly remembered me. In fact, it looks like he was worried that I'd write a story that said he refused to return calls. So, he called my editor at *Long Island Press* to confirm that I actually wrote for the paper. The *Press* vouched for me. I was expecting a call from Ben-Veniste after that; it never came.

After my story was in the can, I got an email from Ben-Veniste. He said that he had never received the videotape of our broadcast, and that he'd need to see it before agreeing to any more media access. I sent him the tape.

To his credit, when Condoleezza Rice was on the stand in Washington on April 4, 2004, Ben-Veniste asked some of the hardest questions of any of the Commissioners. Rice stared at the ceiling, as she answered with insouciant disdain. Her disregard for the Commission masked her lying under oath. When Ben-Veniste began to interrupt her subterfuge and win gallery applause, I felt as proud as a Little League Dad. But when you think of all the anomalies of 9/11, and all the softball questions asked thereof, the Commission's crimes of omission are glaring. The decision to throw a few tough questions at the perjurious Ms. Rice was a no-brainer. Still, it was nice to see a glimpse of the old Watergate prosecutor Ben-Veniste come out from underneath the leathery, corporate, DC-insider stall-technique expert Ben-Veniste.

The Big Wedding:

Because of his self-imposed ban on reporters named Sander Hicks, Ben-Veniste and I didn't meet again until May 19th, 2004. It had been over a year since our "infomercial." The hearings were back in New York City, this time at the New School University buildings on West 12th Street. Homeland Security Chief Tom Ridge came and made jokes. Rudy Giuliani only attempted to make some jokes. It was like a prom. Lots of dressing up, lots of pictures. No tough questions. All the TV cameras were camped outside on West 12th street under tents in the rain, watching the celebrity hearings on small TV sets. Everyone was bored.

After it was all over, I decided to at least try to talk to Richard Ben-Veniste. I'm an alumnus of the New School. I had studied Hegel and Adorno upstairs back in the early '90s and I knew the back exit on West 11th Street. I went around the corner and sure enough, there were the suits, shuffling into Lincoln Town Cars and limos. And there was Richard Ben-Veniste, murmuring to someone on the sidewalk. He was surrounded by aides holding umbrellas over him, as well as by cops.

"Richard Ben-Veniste," I called out when I was close.

He turned slowly.

"Well. San...der. Hicks." He flashed a grin.

I said, "How you doing? Hey I've been trying to get in touch with you. Listen, I was wondering what you thought of the tape I sent."

"It was just as I thought. It confirmed my worst suspicions."

"What's that?"

He grinned again, tight and icy. "You're a whackjob."

And with that, I became the proud recipient of the following award: the only reporter in America to be called names by a member of the National Commission on Terrorist Attacks upon the United States. And it happened in the pouring rain on the grounds of my old school in the West Village.

After being knighted a "whackjob," the aides pressed in closer, and a handler started talking importantly about the limo or something. They began to usher their charge back inside the building. I had about three seconds remaining to get off a return shot. I pulled back and thought of all the prophets throughout history who had focused on one thing—the truth—and made everything else secondary.

I said, "Hey, Richard, you can't just call me a 'whackjob' and walk away like that, after I called you so many times for the paper and you played cat-and-mouse and called my editor but not me. Do you know what this whole thing is?"

At this point, he was back inside, and the glass door was closing. I remembered the thoughts I had when Tom Ridge and Rudy Giuliani had been trotted out before the Commission amid the applause and the cheers. I screamed at the glass wall:

"This is one big PARADE. It's a game of CHARADES. This is all FAKE."

I felt a big hand on my shoulder. NYPD.

"OK. You said your piece, now get out of here."

And I turned and walked out into the cold rain.

Behind me, Richard Ben-Veniste waited in the cool, dry halls of the West 11 Street New School building, the same place where I once learned about the Alien and Sedition Acts and the government's unconstitutional wartime suppression of dissent, the war on the Industrial Workers of the World, and the power of slave autobiographies. Richard Ben-Veniste was hiding in a rare building, a yellow Bauhaus structure that had taught me the bloody truth about history. The irony wasn't lost on me. I left satisfied. I had been true to my old school.

CHAPTER 8

FROM THE GROUND UP:
THE 9/11 TRUTH MOVEMENT

"It's not like I think I'm the greatest investigative reporter in the world. Anyone could have come down here and discovered much of what I found."

—Daniel Hopsicker, from our interview

I suggest to you, my friend, that the interests of those who killed Kennedy now transcend national boundaries and national priorities. No doubt we are dealing now with an international conspiracy. We must face that fact—and not waste any more time micro-analyzing the evidence.

The truth was easily ascertainable. I feel that my work on the assassination is an accomplishment which required little intelligence, minimal analytic ability, and no special talents. Rather, it reflected a willingness to bear witness to the truth irrespective of the consequences. In my responsibility to adhering to the truth as I saw it, I have been and will continue to be, oblivious to all the consequences of its expression.

—Vincent Salandria
Philadelphia Attorney & JFK Researcher

Ah, "The 9/11 Truth Movement."

How can one attempt to describe this fractious, nationwide phenomenon of disparate researchers and activists, spread far and wide, but tied umbilicalally on the web? This amorphous network of folks has only recently become known by such a heavy term as "The 9/11 Truth Movement," and that name is sort of a stretch. This "movement" has displayed a tendency to hinder its work by fragmenting into sharp sects and bitter rivalries. Can loner net junkies unify into truth warriors and turn the tide of history?

At its worst moments, the 9/11 Truth Movement gives one insight into why the term "conspiracy theorist" came to be short-hand for "discredited whacko" in the invisible guidebook of mainstream media. Suddenly, it's not hard to understand why the obvious anomalies in the JFK assassination never received proper attention in accepted media channels. If you have just as many nutty theories about the driver of the limo turning around and shooting JFK as you have honest scientific inquiries about the real probability of multiple shooters, the wheat drowns in the chaff.

Similarly, the 9/11 Truth Movement bears the seeds of its own destruction. At times, the serious questions seem threatened to be drowned by the theories about "pods" being attached to the bottom of the planes, "napalm" being planted in the World Trade Center explosions, "no planes hit the towers," or the real ringer, "Flight 77 was not what hit the Pentagon."

I attended the movement's first national conference in San Francisco in late March 2004. There was a healthy diversity of opinion and many well-researched presentations. But anyone who still believed that Flight 77 crashed into the Pentagon was called an agent of "limited hangout." The term, coined by President Nixon while trying to limit disclosure on Watergate, is always pronounced with a sneer.

But let's start first with the issues that unite the movement. When the Bush Administration lives under a veil of secrecy, theories to explain their collusion and make explicit their conspiracies naturally follow. In order to try and get a pulse on the concerns of the movement, I composed a poll and began to circulate it online. My questions were as follows:

1. If you could ask the entire 9/11 Commission one question, in open session, what would it be?
2. What has been the 9/11 Commission's biggest sin of omission?
3. If you could replace the 9/11 Commission with a three-member panel, who would be on that panel?
4. What's your background before becoming a 9/11 Truth Activist?
5. What other causes are related to 9/11 Truth Activism?

The number of answers I received was not overwhelming, so what follows can't be considered a vastly scientific survey. But, among the twenty or so responses, a pattern emerged. And the quality of the answers was a refreshing surprise. Respondents described themselves as business people, mothers, environmental activists, musicians, information tech, professors of English, and writers. Their answers were intelligent, freethinking, and fearlessly reasoning outside the box of the official story.

"Damn," I thought, "maybe these Don Quixotes will some day be a potent threat, a historical force."

Multiple respondents said the 9/11 Commission's biggest sin of omission was the failure to grill Bush and Cheney under oath, using their subpoena power. Musician Michael Kane said the one question he'd most like to ask the Commission is, "What explanation did George Bush give to you in closed session for his incomprehensible actions on the morning of 9/11?" Derek Davidson pointed out that the Commission has "the power to force officials to testify in public, but instead they have been begging officials." Davidson's burning question to the Commission is, "Why do you keep avoiding questions about the actual day of 9/11/01 as relates to the stand-down of U.S. military jets?"

OTHER QUESTIONS:

"Why did World Trade Center Seven collapse?"

Seven World Trade Center was never hit by any planes. Yet, after an explosive sound, the building collapsed into its own footprint around 5:20 PM on the day of 9/11. The official story from FEMA is that a small fire in the upper reaches of the building probably spread down to fuel tanks in the basement and blew up the whole thing. But even FEMA is not sure that they can back that one up. On May 1, 2002, FEMA wrote in their report, "The specifics of the fires in WTC 7 and how they caused the building to collapse remain unknown at this time." Thanks. Meanwhile, the public is left with the image of the WTC 7 collapsing into its own foundation, and an official story that insults our intelligence.

"Why the fast clean-up of a crime scene?"

All the wreckage and steel from Ground Zero was sold to recyclers and shipped out to China and India, thanks to a quick deal New York City made with two New Jersery companies: Metal Management Northeast and Hugo Neu Schnitzer East, (one of the largest scrap recyclers in the nation) of Jersey City.

"What about the war games being conducted on 9/11?"

English Professor Dr. Jamey Hecht summarizes why the recent revelations about military drills are important to understanding why 9/11 happened on 9/11. "Several simultaneous war games were being run, having been scheduled months in advance. These included Northern Guardian, which tied up so many U.S. fighter aircraft that there were only eight left to protect the Northeastern United States that morning. Another two war games run on the morning of September 11th were Vigilant Warrior (NORAD) and Vigilant Guardian (Joint Chiefs); the first a live-fly "hijacked aircraft" drill using real planes, the second a virtual drill of the same kind. These made it impossible for NORAD and FAA controllers to discern the genuinely hijacked planes and intercept them."

The scheduling of three simultaneous war games on 9/11 certainly explains how the NORAD and FAA could have been caught off guard. But then the question becomes: *how did the terrorists know to strike on 9/11?* These are some well-connected terrorists!

Back to Dr. Hecht: "When the planes hit, I knew the Air Force had been somehow neutralized. Now we know how and by whom." On that day, Hecht "felt a loss begin...it has continued with an urgency and momentum that I attribute to the scope of what was lost: three thousand New Yorkers, half the Constitution, and most of the Republic."

When asked to propose members for a new 9/11 Commission, respondents suggested Former South African President Nelson Mandela, Populist Super-Attorney Gerry Spence, former Bush I Assistant Secretary of Housing Catherine Austin Fitts, and 9/11 Widow Kristin Breitweiser. Congresswoman Cynthia McKinney, and Independent Researcher Mike Ruppert both received multiple nominations. Other suggestions included "pitbull progressive" Congressman Henry Waxman, Senator Ron Paul, and *New Pearl Harbor* author David Ray Griffin.

RELATING TO THE WORLD

After the first set of questions, I posed a new batch, aiming to be more provocative. Here's what I sent out:

"I wanted to ask you about the so-called 9/11 Truth Movement in your town. Does it exist? Has it become an actual movement, or is it just a bunch of folks with shaky credibility? Or has that credibility gone recently from nothing to something? What about the media in your town? Does talk radio talk about it? Is there an Indy Media Center, and do they talk about it?

What about the "Left" in your area? Do they discuss stuff about 9/11?"

These answers were much more reflective. Several times, the answers seem to consider: if we truly have a movement here, what will it take to gain mass support?

While doing background research for my story on Randy Glass, I spoke with Mr. Jon Vincent, who retired from the FBI only last year and is now at Judicial Watch, Chicago. Vincent had been the partner of FBI whistle-blower Robert Wright. Yet, Mr. Vincent is not willing to consider the implications of his former partner's story about the FBI suppressing the bin Laden investigation. Given a quick five-minute summary of the evidence that the Bush White House knew of the 9/11 attacks, did not prevent them, and is trying to cover up the trail, Vincent doesn't deny that the facts seem damning. Yet he's just not willing to entertain any anti-Bush theories. Vincent would "rather go play golf on Saturday and be able to sleep at night," rather than think that the government is complicit in mass murder. The facts are not enough.

Maybe a lifetime in the FBI has desensitized Mr. Vincent. Perhaps you need to be on a different plane to be able to perceive the truth. Demitria Monde Thraam, a San Francisco artist and web designer, says that "Being part of/peripherally connected to the drug subculture for half my life has caused me to already know that our government can and does murder its own...The belief that GWB Co. allowed the attacks is not a belief that many people can literally stand having and still be able to sleep at night...I think this is the major problem we have to deal with, much more important than proving particulars about the event itself (i.e. whether there was or was not a plane hitting the Pentagon, et cetera.)."

The movement is also having a hard time getting the broader "Left" in America interested. Fred Schlange in Chicago wrote, "It is a non-issue in Chicago media...though the student papers at University of Illinois show some interest. The Left in Chicago is still very cautious. Many of us were burned by the Chicago Police Red Squad in the sixties, and we still carry the scars. Literally."

But hope springs eternal in Peoria, Illinois. E-list administrator and truth activist Connie Cook Smith writes, "When I presented my two years of research in Peoria on the second anniversary of 9/11, fifty people came to the talk. That's a small number, but for conservative Peoria, it was considerably more than I expected, out of a population of 112,000—especially since my promos stressed that I would focus on the deceptive aspects of it."

Kezia Jauron connects with a community of over fifty fellow progressive activists in the San Fernando Valley, outside of LA. She reports that "When trying to discuss these issues with mainstream progressives not often caught deep in thought, the attitude toward 9/11 has been 'but regardless...millions of lives have been lost and the whole world is forever changed.' Even though it's thousands, not millions, and probably four-fifths of the world could not give a shit." Other Valley voices have quipped to Jauron, "If you can't get beyond the politics of 9/11, I don't understand your involvement in politics."

But what are the theories inside the 9/11 Truth Movement(s) that Jauron herself finds not credible? "Use of remote control [to pilot the planes]. Individual interviews with rescue workers and debris removal crews proving the results of explosives [referring to the work of Christopher Bollyn[64]]...the report that SF Mayor Willie Brown was told not to fly as of 9/10." Jauron's got a point there. Many have heard that Brown was warned not to fly. It's true, but he didn't take the warning seriously and cancel his flight until he saw the disaster taking place right before leaving for the airport.

Lisa De Witt of Tucson, Arizona, reports, "Most of the news that comes occasionally through the TV or radio about 9/11, I see first on the Internet. One specific example I can think of right off hand is the story about the Saudi flights which took place after 9/11 while everyone else, including Clinton, etc., was grounded. I had read about it as far back as a year or more ago on the Internet. And when the 9/11 Commission finally got around to questioning Clarke, which I watched on CNN, they asked him if he was the one who gave permission for the Saudis to leave the country. Still, there is a lot of stuff that doesn't make it into the mainstream news, like the Sibel Edmonds story." DeWitt is making reference to the former FBI translator who is fast becoming a thorn in the side of the Bush Justice Department. She was stopped from translating Al Qaeda-related documents at the FBI. Her story, first reported by Gail Sheehy in *New York Observer*, revealed an alarming penetration of the FBI translating department by pro-terrorist factions. Rather than investigate Edmonds' documented allegations, then-Attorney General Ashcroft took the unprecedented step of issuing a gag-order on Edmonds, by invoking the seldom-used "State Secrets Law." Ashcroft issued an almost ridiculous order that "classified" the already public-domain material related to Edmonds.

64 Bollyn writes for the right-leaning *American Free Press* and did do some commendable work on the mysterious October 2002 plane crash of Senator Paul Wellstone, as cited in Vox Pop's title, *American Assassination: The Strange Death of Senator Paul Wellstone.*

The Big Wedding:

DeWitt recommends everyone read Edmonds in her own words. Before being silenced Edmonds accused Ashcroft, the singing "Soaring Eagle" himself, of hiding "serious criminal activities" and "complicity in covering up."[65]

In Texas, Al Rogers reports that in the "People's Republic of Austin, the left here seems to be disinterested in 9/11 truth-seeking. I've signed up for local '9/11 meetups', but they get cancelled because they can't even get the minimum five people to sign up. This is surprising to me, because the Austin Public Access TV schedule includes at least five weekly shows that discuss the 9/11 conspiracy on a regular basis. The hosts are intelligent and informative, but are mostly approaching the topic from a conservative/Christian perspective."

Baltimore Financial Advisor Jim Funck also reports, "I had not heard of the 9/11 truth movement. A quick look up on the internet shows three people signed up in Baltimore."

The news is better from Savannah, Georgia, where New York Green Party activist Mitchell Cohen helped organize a successful "People's 9/11 Truth Commission" march and press conference at the G8 protests, reporting they got "Lots of radio and TV coverage." Cohen opines: "marches in small towns across the country will garner much more publicity than trying to do splashy events in NY or San Francisco."

Maybe Cohen's right. When I spoke alongside UN arms inspector Scott Ritter and 9/11 Widow Ellen Mariani in late May at the Riverside Church, the leaders of NY 9/11 Truth had high expectations. They wanted to pack the gigantic hall and be able to say they had drawn 1,500 people. When a decent six hundred attended, they took that as a sign of failure. Yet, the event got great press coverage in print and on radio, and helped legitimize the cause in the media capital of the USA.

Adam Hurter of Amherst, Massachusetts deserves an award for the most succinct, eloquent and inspirational bit of prose in the entire poll:

"Most people, including Leftists, are scared of the notion of conspiracy. It's hard and scary to swallow that an organized gang of powerful capitalists within our own country killed the president in 1963 and then organized September 11 four decades later. It happens to be true. And much of the institutional Left is denying the reality. It's the reality that has the potential to bring people together in recognition of our common enemy, the fascist/capitalist force that is dominating the world. The Truth is

<hr />

65 For more on this, Edmonds, and the emergent National Security Whistle-blowers Coalition see http://www.justcitizen.com

the force that has the most genuine revolutionary potential."

Closer to home, he reports that there is a small organized 9/11 Truth Movement in Northampton/Amherst, about a half-dozen folks. They have held a couple of rallies, and are planning to bring 9/11 widow Ellen Mariani to town. Although no local media cover 9/11 questions in the area, copies of *The New Pearl Harbor* are flying out of bookstores.

Back to Adam Hurter: "A big part of the problem is that there are countless 'red herrings' out there: false or distracting stories and information about 9/11. When people see information that was used against the official story turn out to be untrue, the credibility of the whole conspiracy stance is weakened in their minds. People should be encouraged to consider the implausibility of the official story itself."

Recall that Monde in San Francisco laid out the core problem: He effectively said that in a movement obsessed with making a scientific, unassailable, meticulous argument, we get ourselves caught in a maze. If we can't relate to people where they are, with more than just cerebral data, we're not going to be able to create a massive paradigm shift. Michael Moore's *Fahrenheit 9/11* touches the same nerve here—the point at which people have to decide to feel, or overcome their own fear enough to understand that Bush and Company are suspects in domestic-mass murder.

To Monde, and I, this is more of a challenge than "proving particulars about the event itself."

RED HERRINGS

The no-plane-hit-the-Pentagon theory was first advanced by Thierry Meyssan, in two books he first published in France: *The Horrible Fraud,* and then, in the follow-up, *Pentagate.* Due to the lack of evidence left by the wreckage, the flight pattern of the plane, and the lack of security video footage, the theory goes: American Airlines Flight 77 did not hit the Pentagon. Instead, it was probably a smaller plane or a cruise missile.

On the other side of the argument are people like John Judge, director of 9/11 Citizens Watch, and Penny Schoner. The former personally knows a female flight attendant who was regularly on Flight 77. Visiting the wreckage, she was shocked to find a bracelet that once belonged to her friend. (This is not the only odd coincidence in 9/11 lore. Widow Kristen Breitweiser was unable to recover any of her late husband's Ron's remains from the WTC except for his ring finger, still wearing their wedding ring).

Penny Schoner is a colleague of Judge's, and has published a booklet called *American Airline #77 Hit the Pentagon on 9/11/01*. Spiral bound and self-published, the book includes eighty-six eyewitnesses, most of whom saw the American flight actually make impact with the Pentagon. I bought a copy from Schoner at the conference in San Francisco. Priced at twenty dollars, the full color photos made it totally worth it.

Part of Meyssan's theory is that the nose cone of the plane could not have penetrated three layers of the Pentagon, and have made such a small distinct hole in the third. At the street level, most proponents of the theory (most of whom obviously haven't read Meyssan's book) believe that his theory is that the original hole on the outside of the Pentagon was too small for a 757 to have caused it. After reading Schoner's booklet and viewing her pictures, I realize something: part of the problem is the image that has come to be associated with *Pentagate*, and Meyssan's entire theory, is this one:

Yet that photo is admittedly inside, on the third layer of the Pentagon (but on the front cover of *Pentagate*).

There is a wealth of other photos that should be weighed in the balance with this theory, such as:

This photo, and countless others like it don't appear on the most "out-there" 9/11 conspiracy websites, because there's an over-imaginative, ultra-radical element in this movement that believes that the more outlandish the theory, the better. Anything is possible. Nothing is true. This is poison for something that aspires to be a "movement."

Professor Jim Fetzer teaches logic at the University of Minnesota in Duluth. He's an expert on the murder of JFK, having edited and written three books.[66] I asked him about the use of "red herrings" in the cover-up on the JFK hit. How have independent researchers been deliberately thrown off the trail in the past?

> *"Setting up Oswald as a pro-Castro communist sympathizer was a major red herring, intended to send investigators off in the wrong direction. The FBI, the Warren Commission, Naval officers, agents of the Secret Service, members of the press, were all used to disseminate disinformation."*

Thierry Meyssan is a president of Reseau Voltaire, a left wing activist network and think tank, and is also National Secretary of the "Radical Left" Party (PRG). I don't mean to imply here that Meyssan is fomenting disinformation on behalf of the U.S. National Security State. Perhaps his Pentagon theory was just a notion from left-field that Meyssan happened to put on paper. But it certainly has found an audience in the movement. At the San Francisco conference, the "no plane" theory was discussed as if it were a proven fact. If there was any dissent, none of the organizers gave it a forum.

But, for the sake of argument here, let's consider that John Judge and Penny Schoner are correct, that the no plane theory is just a distraction. It certainly is an effective way to discredit the movement. For example, let's look at the classic swing voter by interviewing my mother, Mrs. Ann-Marie Hicks.

Mom's a right-leaning "independent" who voted for Reagan, Bush I, and Bush II. She's vocal, stubborn, and fiercely anti-abortion. She's also passionate and active in local foodbank, anti-poverty charities. She was a Bush supporter without fail until the *London Daily Mail* favorably reviewed the first 9/11 skeptics book, David Ray Griffin's *The New Pearl Harbor.* Then, mom saw *Fahrenheit 9/11,* and temporarily withdrew her support for Bush. She planned to vote for Kerry/Edwards. But what about 9/11? Are the theories that she once dismissed as "kooky" now more considerable?

"No."

Why not?

"I know two people who saw the PLANE (not a missile) go into the Pentagon."

66 Dr. Fetzer is also co-author of the book I edited on the death of Minnesota Senator Paul Wellstone, *American Assassination.*

The entire 9/11 Truth Movement is dismissed by its most outlandish theory. The 9/11 argument is a chain of logic, and in this chain there is a conspicuously weak link. Mom happens to live within ten miles of the Pentagon, and she knows a priest and a friend's daughter who saw the plane hit.

How can this movement advance when people who are skeptical and smart find an unacceptably illogical theory? They will be turned off, and run from the entire inquiry. If there's one theory out there that is obviously false, the masses can be kept in intellectual submission, because the official story will represent safety, validation, and freedom from ridicule. *The 9/11 Commission Report* acts as a kind of co-dependent parent, offering the promise of comfort and reinforcing the big family lie. The architects of disinformation take it as given that people fear ridicule.

Back to Demitria Monde Thraam in San Fran: "The 'Pentagon missile' issue cannot be directly proven—I used to believe it, but realized it didn't matter as much as the fact that whatEVER hit the Pentagon hit it in that one little sector being renovated at the time. I am also beginning to see the WTC 7 issue as being a possible distraction—most folks would easily accept demolition of a nearby building as a safety measure, whether it was actually done so for that reason or not. We need to focus on what is known, obvious, and impossible to refute."

A new documentary surfaced in early 2004 that advanced one of the more "out there" theories: that the planes that crashed into the WTC had "pods" attached to their underbellies. The cheaply produced, but well-packaged, "9/11 in Plane Sight" is atrociously reasoned and fact-free. It's reliant on a few blurry photographs and a lot of enthusiasm. This is theorizing by the eager. This is what you get when you ignore the effects of globalization, or the reality of rageful Islamic reaction to U.S. foreign policy.

There are over one hundred eyewitnesses who saw Flight 77 descend and crash into the Pentagon. One of them, Johanna Klein, happens to be an old family friend of mine. It took a while for Johanna to get over the trauma of witnessing the tragedy, but eventually she was willing to talk to me about it:

> *"I worked at the time at USA Today, which was in one of the two buildings that were considered the twin towers of Roslyn, in Arlington. And my office, well I didn't have an office, but I worked up on the, I think it was the 21st floor. So, we were pretty high. And shortly after I got to work, I got a phone call from one of the salespeople I worked for who had actually traveled up to*

New York and was in New York at the time. And had told me about what had just happened with the planes. And so we all kind of quickly learned about what had happened in New York. And everyone gathered in the senior vice president's office, which was in the corner, and basically all of her outside walls were lined with windows.

"So you can have a view of basically all of the monuments including the Pentagon, which was, I don't know, maybe a mile away. You're up so high you can definitely see everything. So there were probably twenty of us packed into her office watching the big TV that she had in there on the news.

"And one of the things they had said on the news was that they had shut down all plane activity in and out of the major cities. And I guess, just by instinct, all of us turned and looked out the window for confirmation of that because given that we work so close to a national airport we constantly saw planes flying by our windows all the time. So we all turned to look out at that point and I saw a plane and I actually, it didn't hit me at the time what the plane was doing. So I was like, yeah right, look at that, look at that plane, but I stopped mid-sentence because I realized at that time that the plane was basically nose-diving and going very, very, very fast toward the ground.

"We probably saw the last four to five seconds of its flight, and then it just exploded into a major fireball."

EPILOGUE

Jan Hoyer of 9/11 Visibility made a silent movie about handing out 9/11 pamphlets and rambling in the working class sections of Kansas City outside punk shows and bodegas. The camera catches the different reactions to a dedicated activist handing out information. There's something oddly poetic and wistful about a silent movie on trying to inform the entire public in a big city in the breadbasket. Something about the Midwest and wheat strikes me as pure and hopeful and admirable.

Kansas City 9/11 Visibility holds protest vigils every Saturday. If Kansas City is indicative of what's going on in the rest of the country, the movement certainly goes through a lot. Jan Hoyer and his friends have been shoved by the manager at the local Barnes & Noble, attacked by a twenty-five-year-old "Rush Limbaughite," and closely monitored by police after attending church services in a minority neighborhood. In

February, they braved subzero cold to hand candidate John Edwards the famous "deception dollar," a flyer with key 9/11 websites, dressed up to look like an oversized greenback. In Edwards case, he accepted the deception dollar and in exchange gave his "trademark boyish smile on command."

When an amped-up, right-wing twenty-five-year-old ditto-head started screaming in their faces at a protest vigil, Kansas City Bob simply sang a little hymn in response, "Let There Be Peace On Earth and Let It Begin With Me." Finally, a police officer arrived and talked to the lad about the Constitution. It took an hour. Then, the boy came back to the protestors, apologized for earlier saying "America will never be safe until you are removed from the streets," and walked away.

Down in Southern Maryland, the "undiscovered suburb," twenty miles south of D.C., lives Evan West, an old friend from high school. He teaches freshman English in a small town where he lives with his wife and two children. I asked Evan how the 9/11 Truth Movement is doing in Bryans Road, Maryland.

"The liberal fringe and most of the black community have no problem believing that Bush could have had something to do with 9/11. To them, it is just another byproduct of the corrupt, white male machine that has conspired to oppress for hundreds of years."

"I know that Bush and his cronies are liars. I know that they use a far right religious ideology to justify their amoral actions. I'm just not quite ready to say that they had a hand in killing three thousand innocent people."

Just you wait, Evan. Once this 9/11 Truth Movement works out a few kinks, it's going to be unstoppable. *The Truth is the force that has the most genuine revolutionary potential.*

When I asked Green Party Brooklynite Mitchell Cohen, "Is there any one theory or branch of the 9/11 Truth Movement you find more credible than others? Any that are less credible?"

He said, "No comment. We are all working extremely hard to unearth the Truth."

CHAPTER 9

MUSLIM BROTHERHOOD, TEAM B, PNAC, AND THE NEW INTERNATIONAL FASCIST AGENDA

Your face was blue in the light of the screen
As we watched the speech of an animal scream.
The new party army
was marching right over our heads.

There you are, ha, ha, I told you so,
hurrah, trala,
Says everybody that we know, hurrah, trala!
But who hid a radio under the stairs?
Who got caught out unawares
When the new party army came marching right over our heads?

When Johnny comes marching home again, hurrah, trala
Nobody understands it can happen again, hurrah, trala!
The sun is shining
and the kids are shouting loud,
But you gotta know it's shining through a crack in the cloud,
And the shadow keeps falling,
when Johnny comes marching home!

    — "English Civil War"
Joe Strummer and the Clash

Nobody understands that it can happen again. Joe Strummer was talking about a new police state, a resurgent fascism, a new era of fear he prophesied would be ushered in, in the wake of a televised spectacle. And although plenty of good people have spoken out against the trampling of the Bill of Rights under the banner of "Homeland Security," no one has explored the connections "Al Qaeda" has to an international neo-fascist agenda.

Lets explore where this new term "Al Qaeda" came from, and why the force that people normally describe as "Al Qaeda" is more accurately described by the words "Muslim Brotherhood," "Islamic Jihad," "Hamas," or even "Team B."

AL QAEDA

Former National Security Advisor Richard Clarke described Al Qaeda as "...part of an international political network...hiding behind a religious sect."[67] American culture (with its Christian foundations rooted deep in the dominant subconscious) tends to identify Al Qaeda as devotees of the "other" religion, Islam. But Clarke's suggestion here is that the religious aspects of the movement are a disguise.

Let's take that analysis one step further. Where did the name "Al Qaeda" come from? It's a relative newcomer to the international lexicon, supposedly the invention of the moderate Mujahedeen leader Abdullah Azzam in 1989. Yet it didn't appear in the U.S. media until 1996, and it didn't gain traction until after the August 1998 Embassy bombings.

"Al Qaeda" is a curious choice for the name of a revolutionary group: literally it means "the base" but it can also imply "the bottom," "the anus," or something having to do with menstruation. The Arabic root word is "qaf-ayn-dal." It can mean a camp or a home, a foundation; but also a rule, principle, formula, or method. It's been suggested that Azzam, the spiritual mentor to bin Laden, "was talking about a mode of activism and a tactic, not talking about a particular organization."[68]

According to Montreal professor R.T. Naylor:

> "Al Qaeda itself does not exist, except in the fevered imaginations of neo-cons and Likudniks, some of whom, I suspect, also know it is a myth, but find it extremely useful as a bogeyman to spook the public and the politicians to acquiesce in otherwise unacceptable policy initiatives at home and abroad. By those terms, Al Qaeda is cast like 'the Mafia' and similar nonsense coming from police lobbies."[69]

Top BBC documentarian Adam Curtis broadcast his three-part television film "The Power of Nightmares," in early 2005 on

---

67 Richard A. Clarke, *Against All Enemies* (New York: Free Press, 2004)
68 http://www.twf.org/News/Y2003 /0622-Qaeda.html
69 From interview by Standard Schaefer http://www.counterpunch.org/schafer06212003.html

British TV, and pointed out the similarities between "Al Qaeda" and the American neo-conservative agenda. Both are willing to use religion as propaganda, while ignoring the moral principles at the core of the respective faiths. Both worked together to fight the Soviets in Afghanistan. Both headed off in separate directions after the Mujahedeen civil war, but with a full head of steam and a strategy of violence and rule-by-fear. In both cases, that strategy didn't result in the massive followings both movements longed for. Curtis points out that the Islamists then turned to terrorism, in a desperate and doomed attempt to win the people over to their side. Likewise, the neo-cons also thrive off this same terrorism, because fighting it justifies their existence.

MUSLIM BROTHERHOOD

logo of Muslim Brotherhood

Curtis's documentary is laudable. But he states that the term "Al Qaeda" is not the most accurate, without suggesting what terms are better. How should we refer to the organizational force of the Islamists that seeks to destroy the USA and create a global theocracy? That would be the Muslim Brotherhood, in Arabic, "Al-Ikhwan Al-Moslemoon." The Brotherhood is a social, political network that ties together the political Right, the Nazis, the neo-cons, and Al Qaeda.

Muslim Brotherhood was started in 1928 in Egypt and has been involved in a variety of terrorist activities since (including the assassination of Egyptian President Anwar Sadat, and an earlier attempt on President Gamal Abdel-Nasser). Yet, it's not on the U.S. Treasury's watch list of terrorist organizations. Its history is mentioned, briefly, in *The 9/11 Commission Report*, buried in the 11th endnote of Chapter 2. When the *Washington Post* and *Wall Street Journal* reported on it, they didn't mention the well-documented links to wealthy neo-Nazis. The *Washington Post* did, however, quote a "former" CIA official who called the Brotherhood "the preeminent movement in the Muslim world... something we can work with." He warned that to alienate the organization "would be foolhardy in the extreme." [70] According to the *Post*, the CIA relies on the Brotherhood for intelligence.

---

70 John Mintz and Douglas Farah, "U.S. Hopes to Work With Diverse Group," *Washington Post* September 11, 2004.

"Mastermind of Terror" Khalid Sheikh Mohammed joined the Muslim Brotherhood at age sixteen. Mohammed Atta's father is a member, and researchers are almost certain that Atta himself was one as well. Atta was a member of a Muslim Brotherhood "unofficial base" when he joined an engineer's syndicate after studying architecture at Cairo University in 1990. Amanda Keller remembers Atta using the term of endearment "Brother" for his companion in Venice, Marwan Al-Shehhi, but not other Arabs. One of the Germans who partied with them in Key West, "Stephen," was also a "Brother."[71]

The Muslim Brotherhood was founded by a young Egyptian schoolteacher Hassan Banna. Banna railed against colonialism and argued for a government based on the Koran. The Brotherhood grew quickly, with a militia, oaths of allegiance, and a culture of secrecy. The Brotherhood worked for Third Reich intelligence before and during World War II. Banna was assassinated by the Egyptian state in 1949. Although the Brotherhood facilitated the rise to power of President Nasser, Nasser turned out to be committed to a secular state. When the Brotherhood made an attempt on his life, Nasser clamped down and imprisoned them by the thousands. Similar repression took place against the group's tentacles in Iraq and Syria.

Sayyid Qutb, the Egyptian writer and fierce proselytizer, was a Muslim Brother, and a big influence on Osama bin Laden. His commitment to violence and terror were deepened by his experiences in Egyptian prison, where he was covered in animal fat and thrown into a cell full of attack dogs. He was hanged in 1966.

The Brotherhood split into two divisions in 1953, a militant and a political branch, the latter of which eventually elected some of its own to the Egyptian parliament. This is ironic, because this brand of Islam believes that democracy and representative government are contrary to the will of Allah. They believe that only a government built on sharia, or Islamic law, is justifiable. The stated platform of the Muslim Brotherhood is to ban national elections, once they actually win one.

Mahrous bin Laden, older brother of Osama, was close to certain Syrians who were militant Muslim Brothers. When the Brotherhood denounced the Saudi royal family and seized Mecca's Grand Mosque in 1979, Mahrous was found partly at fault. The Brotherhood had used Bin Laden Construction company trucks to slip the militants past security.

Today, the government of Syria is trying to ferret the

71 As mentioned earlier, Daniel Hopsicker identified "Brother" Stephen as Stephen Verhaaren, owner of a Naples, Florida aviation company. In return, Verhaaren sued Hopsicker. I spoke with Verhaaren on the phone as this book was going to press. He denied knowing Atta, or being a member of Muslim Brotherhood. I thought the conversation was pleasant, but later, his lawyer later said his client was "upset" by the call.

Muslim Brotherhood out of their country. Before the 2003 U.S. invasion of Iraq, the CIA's Robert Baer was on the verge of getting the Syrians to provide a list of Muslim Brotherhood members, worldwide. They offered this list of real terrorists on the condition that the U.S. reconsider its attack on non-terrorist Saddam Hussein. After all, Hussein hadn't been behind 9/11, the Muslim Brotherhood had. A logical deal? Not to the White House, who refused it.

Still wondering why Muslim Brotherhood is not on the U.S. Treasury's list of terrorist organizations? Recall that double agent Ali Mohammed was active in one of the Muslim Brotherhood's most militant fronts, Egyptian Islamic Jihad. This helps explain why the CIA is reporting favorable things about the group via the willing vessel of the *Washington Post*. Muslim Brotherhood is also the financial and organizational backbone of not only Al Qaeda, but also Hamas and Palestinian Islamic Jihad.

Muslim Brotherhood's name commonly comes up in mainstream channels as an offhand reference to the organizers of Mujahedeen resistance in Afghanistan. By 1979, Muslim Brotherhood was active in about forty countries, and was able to recruit soldiers into the struggle worldwide. According to Rita Katz in *Terrorist Hunter*, the Muslim Brotherhood first established a front in the U.S. in 1973 with the Islamic Association (IA), later called IAP (Islamic Association for Palestine). This association funneled funds from U.S. donors into Muslim Brotherhood's Maktab al Khidamat (MAK) Mujahedeen "support services" group in Pakistan, run by Osama bin Laden with the help of the CIA. According to former federal prosecutor John Loftus, Vice President Bush "was in charge of the covert operations that supported the MAK."[72]

Rita Katz and my SEC contact both report an alarming number of Muslim Brotherhood affiliated non-profit organizations permitted to operate in the U.S.: among them are the American Muslim Council and the Council on American Islamic Relations. Only after intense outside pressure did the Feds arrest two board members of these groups in 2003: Sami al-Arian, in February, and Abdulrahman Alamoudi, in September. Both were close to President Bush and had helped the White House create an image of benevolent Islamic-American relations. Both groups met with Karl Rove in 2001 to help with the White House's faith-based initiatives, and Sami al-Arian campaigned for Bush in Florida. When Alamoudi was arrested, there were "vehement protests and interference at FBI HQ"

72 Craig Unger, *House of Bush, House of Saud* (New York: Scribner, 2004)

according to my SEC contact. When Sami al-Arian was taken down, he was charged with conspiracy to commit murder, since he supported and helped fund suicide attacks in Israel. According to government officials, al-Arian is a top dog at Muslim Brotherhood's branch office, the Palestinian Islamic Jihad.

Al-Arian obviously felt he had protection from above. How did he make the cut as a friend of President Bush?

Saudi money.

Sami al-Arian was not busted until John Loftus filed a suit against him in Florida court in 2002 (Loftus is somewhat legendary in publishing circles for detailing Prescott Bush's Nazi dealings on Wall Street, in *The Secret War Against the Jews*. Bush raised $50 million for Adolph Hitler's Third Reich). According to Loftus, "The Saudi government was laundering money through Florida charities run by University of Southern Florida Professor Sami al Arian for the support of terrorist groups in the Middle East." My SEC contact pointed out, "Terrorist money-mover Sami Al-Arian was so effective in Florida, the fifty thousand Muslims who had traditionally voted Democrat overwhelmingly swung Republican. Bush also received campaign support from Khaled Elgindy, who headed the Texas cause, and George Salem, who headed national efforts from Washington, DC in 2000."

The Saudi government officially cut off support to the Muslim Brotherhood when the group condemned them for allowing U.S. bases on Saudi soil, in 1990. But evidence persists that the Saudis continued support for Muslim Brotherhood's Gaza strip branch, Hamas.[73] In 1994, when a Saudi defector Mohammed al-Khilewi (first secretary at the Saudi Mission to the UN) wanted to give the FBI fourteen thousand documents that proved Saudi funding of Hamas, the FBI refused to accept them.[74]

My SEC contact has been tracking the Muslim Brotherhood for a while: "My task force work for SEC Chicago began in 1999 (following international banks), as Rita Katz was tasked to cover non-profits.... I was tasked with others to explore manipulation and control of securities markets."

And what have you learned of Muslim Brotherhood?

"They worked for Ibn Saud to help him unite Arabia, they worked for British intelligence, they worked for French intelligence, they work for U.S. intelligence, a mercenary band 'hiding behind Islam' which

Sami al-Arian

---

73 According to the July 2003, Senate Governmental Affairs Committee testimony of Dr. Dore Gold, President, Jerusalem Center for Public Affairs, "The Hamas-Saudi connection should not come as a surprise. Hamas emerged in 1987 from the Gaza branch of Muslim Brotherhood which, as noted earlier, has become a key Saudi ally during previous decades....Saudi Arabia today funds more than 50 percent of the needs of Hamas."

74 Greg Palast, *The Best Democracy Money Can Buy* (New York: Plume, 2004)

is why most of them are cokeheads and alcoholics who simply agitate to attract any psycho or disaffected they can to their ranks." The big question has been, for whom are they working? And the answer seems to be the transnational Reich movement."

The Reich movement. The Nazis. The neo-Nazis. The far right neo-cons. The New Fascists.

Hold onto your seats. There's proof.

MUSLIM BROTHERHOOD AND THE NEO-NAZIS

Yousef Nada

According to the Southern Poverty Law Center, "the financial heart of the Islamist economic apparatus," is a Swiss bank called "Al Taqwa," Arabic for "Fear of God." Al Taqwa was originally founded in 1988 in the Bahamas. One of its main players, Yousef Nada, had served Hitler's Third Reich as an intelligence agent. A member of Muslim Brotherhood, Nada helped Muhammed Amin al-Husseini, the "Grand Mufti" of Jerusalem, escape from Germany to Palestine at the end of WWII. Hussseini had held the rank of Major in the SS, and recruited twenty-six thousand Arabs to fight with the SS in Europe.

According to European money-laundering expert Ernest Backes, Francois Genoud was another ex-spy for the Nazis who was a key part of the formation of Al Taqwa. Although he was a Swiss citizen, at the fall of Berlin, Genoud helped distribute Nazi funds. He was so high up in the Third Reich, that he became the literary heir to the writings of Hitler and Goebbels.

When bank Al Taqwa was raided the November after 9/11, it was thought to hold all known Al Qaeda funds. However, this raid didn't staunch the flow of funds to Islamic terror, and it didn't stop Al Taqwa. On March 20, 2002, in suburban Washington DC, a joint task force raided the SAAR Network, a gaggle of over-lapping Islamic charities. "They hit a bunch of institutions and individuals that were linked with bank Al Taqwa," said radio journalist, on-air host, and leading anti-fascist researcher David Emory, in our interview.[75]

Finally, the government is doing its job and busting the bad guys. Right? Maybe not. Terrorism expert Rita Katz observed a high level of harassment when she participated in the SAAR investigation:

---

75 Dave Emory's radio show can be heard on several stations nation-wide, and is archived online at www.spitfirelist.com.

> *"The CIA was investigating me and the SAAR investigators from Green-quest and Customs. The CIA and the FBI investigated everyone who had anything to do with the SAAR investigation. White vans and SUV's with dark windows appeared near all the homes of the SAAR investigators. All agents, some of whom were very experienced with surveillance, knew they were being followed. So was I. I felt that I was being followed everywhere and watched, at home, in the supermarket, on the way to work...and for what?...I don't know for certain what's the deal with the CIA investigating the SAAR investigators, but it sure feels as if someone up in that agency doesn't like the idea that the Saudi Arabian boat is rocked."[76]*

Clinton White House National Security Council aides first urged an investigation of the SAAR Network, in 1998. But the FBI refused. Their reason? The *Washington Post* reported that "the FBI declined because of fears that a probe would be seen as ethnic profiling." I have to wonder if the *Washington Post* and the FBI are secretly stifling hard laughter. "Ethnic profiling?" This is the same FBI that harassed the Black Panthers into early graves, the same FBI who told Martin Luther King he should go commit suicide. "Ethnic profiling" is a polite, PC excuse, when really the truth has got to be closer to this: the FBI had a severe unwillingness to disturb the money flow of an Islamic charity with connections to the Saudis, and the Far Right.

Once again, the FBI acts like the little brother following orders of the fatter, stronger, colder, aloof CIA. Their "negligence" had serious, direct effects. Even two neo-Nazis seem to have had foreknowledge of the 9/11 disaster.

Ahmed Huber, a Swiss neo-Nazi who converted to Islam, fell under sway of the Grand Mufti when he was in the Middle East. Huber was also a protégé of Johann Von Leers, who had produced Anti-Semitic propaganda under Joseph Goebbels. After the fall of Berlin, Von Leers took a gang of Nazis with him when he moved to Egypt and changed his name to Omar. Von Leers worked for Nasser, as did over one hundred former German military and intelligence personnel who Nasser asked the CIA to find for him. According to David Emory, Huber is:

"Ahmed" Huber

> *"very active on the European New Right scene, and is an intimate of the NPD, the German neo-Nazi party. Huber is something of a bridge between the old Nazis (Genoud, who he met on a daily basis, and Von Leers) and some of the new guard. Also a bridge between the Islamists and the neo-Nazis."*

76 Rita Katz, *Terrorist Hunter* (New York: CCC: 2003) Katz is Director of the SITE Institute, and has briefed Congressional and White House personnel on terrorism issues.

The Big Wedding:

In the U.S., Huber has had a relationship with the New Black Panther Party and Khallid Mohammad. He claims an intimacy with key Al Qaeda personnel. He's such a part of Al Taqwa that his home was raided as part of the Swiss raid on it. According to trackingthethreat.com, Huber "was given advance warning that something big was going to happen here-well before 9/11."[77]

That kind of foreknowledge is very similar to that of William Pierce, the late founder of the North American neo-Nazi group National Alliance. In 1998, Pierce gave a radio address titled "Stay Out of Tall Buildings" that included the these instructions: "New Yorkers who work in tall office buildings anything close to the size of the World Trade Center might consider wearing hard hats."[78]

Maybe that's just loose talk from right wing whackos. But recall that Muslim Brother Ramzi Yousef started planning 9/11 in 1993.

NEO-NAZIS AND BUSH

While we're on the topic of the National Alliance, let's probe further into the relationship between political power in the U.S. and so-called "fringe" groups on the right wing. I was a part of the August 2002 street melee with the National Alliance as part of the confrontational protest against their agenda, as they rallied on Capitol Hill. As part of the preparations for that protest, I created a working paper on some of President Bush's connections to "Southern Heritage" and other white supremacist movements. Here's what I found:

In 1996, Bush sent letters of support to the United Daughters of the Confederacy, praising it for its "dedication to others" and for the group's "high standards." His letter was published in their official magazine in 1996. The Daughters are a historical preservationist group that erects statues to honor the Southern secession. But it's not everybody's history at stake here—they have worked with and honored the pro-Klan, white supremacist scholar Michael A. Grissom.

As Governor of Texas, Bush opposed "hate crimes" legislation, even after the brutal murder of James Byrd who was chained and dragged to death by racist thugs.

In 1997, Governor Bush was a donor to the Museum of the Confederacy's Annual Ball, in Richmond, Virginia. He was named Honorary Chairman at an archaic spectacle where

77 trackingthethreat.com describes itself as an "open source threat network database."
78 View hokey 19th century paintings and the fascist remembrances of Pierce at ttp://www.nationalvanguard.org/story.php?id=3771

guests arrived in traditional period "Confederate" costume. The event was held in the old Tredegar Iron Works, where slave labor was used to make half of the total cannon of the Confederacy.[79]

During the 2000 Presidential campaign, Bush had no problem with the flying of the Confederate Flag over the South Carolina Statehouse. To him, it was an issue for the people of South Carolina to decide. After losing the New Hampshire Primary to McCain by eighteen points, Bush reinvigorated his troops by attacking McCain from South Carolina's Bob Jones University, the far-right Fundamentalist Christian school. The choice of location is telling. Bob Jones University did not official-ly admit minorities until 1975, after a court order brought on by a lawsuit from the IRS. BJU lost their tax-exempt status for out-lawing interracial dating. Attacking McCain from Bob Jones University was a perfect way for Bush to re-invigorate his base and show his donors that ethics would not stop him from capturing the White House for them no matter what.[80] Right around this time, rumors started flying that McCain had fathered a child out of wedlock with an African-American mother.

As president, Bush authorized the placement of a Presidential wreath at the Confederate Monument on Memorial Day 2001. Ironically, Papa Bush had suspended this practice during his own administration.[81]

Even more alarming is the neo-fascist-like behavior of former Attorney General John Ashcroft—in 1998 he supported the pro-slavery magazine *Southern Partisan*, in print. Among the many backward, far-right lunatic beliefs of this magazine are praise for Lincoln's assassin, and "superhero" Nathan Bedford Forrest, founder of the KKK. Ashcroft, in an interview said, "Your magazine also helps set the record straight. You've got a heritage of doing that, of defending Southern patriots.... Traditionalists must do more. I've got to do more."[82]

In Campaign 2000, Bush's Presidential candidacy was offi-cially endorsed by Matt Hale, founder of the far-right Church of the Creator. Five years later, Bush seems even more fascistic: he relishes his two post-9/11 wars, those two genocidal assaults on civilian populations. Although the peoples of Iraq and Afghanistan are not the stated targets of the U.S. military, the amount of civilians killed in the U.S. bombing of Afghanistan surpassed that of 9/11. In fact, as reported in the *New York Times International*, a team of doctors and independent researchers at the Bloomberg School of Public Health at Johns Hopkins University who conducted a study in Iraq, concluded

79 Sources: Chris Kromm's feature on this topic in *Southern Exposure*, also, Richmond National Parks Quarterly Newsletter, and the original introduction to Soft Skull Press's edition of *Fortunate Son* by Nick Mamatas and Toby Rogers.
80 Source: Personal notes from Campaign 2000. See an archived press release on this at Doug Henwood's site, here.
81 Confederate.org
82 Southern Partisan, Second Quarter, 1998

that an estimated one hundred thousand civilians have died in Iraq "as direct or indirect consequences of the March 2003 United States-led invasion."[83]

TEAM B

To some, the Messiah Complex that President Bush clearly suffers from is alarming. He claims that the voice of God told him to attack Iraq despite the lack of a reason. It's widely believed that Bush thinks God put him in the White House to fight the "War on Terror." When he landed on the aircraft carrier USS Lincoln on May 2, 2003, he quoted from the Book of Isaiah, Chapter 61. Being a fundamentalist, he must have known that was the same passage that Jesus of Nazareth quoted in the temple, according to *Luke*, Chapter 4, in order to make the claim that he was the Messiah.

There is a class of men behind Bush who aren't exactly into the Spirit. It's likely they regard Bush's literal evangelical Christianity with amusement. They regard religion as one of Plato's "noble lies." They take to heart what Thomas Hobbes said about ethics and religion—there's no central truth to any of it, but it's a good thing to teach the young.

Karl Rove and his crowd are avowed readers of the vicious strategist Machiavelli: their ideal Prince must "lie and be able to disguise his character well...to be a great feigner and dissembler...be all mercy, faith, integrity, humanity and religion. And nothing is more necessary than to seem to have this last quality...Everybody sees what you are, few feel what you are."[84]

In 1972, Richard Nixon actually displayed virtue by moving the country away from a culture of Cold War paranoia. He signed the Strategic Arms Limitation Talks (SALT) agreement. Nixon sought to curb the massive waste of the arms race through a broad agreement of "détente" with the USSR. This policy made the right wing of the GOP go mad.

In the wake of Watergate, and Nixon's 1974 expulsion from the White House, President Ford faced a challenge from the Republican hawks. In 1976, Dick Cheney was Ford's Chief of Staff and Donald Rumsfeld was, then as now, Secretary of Defense. In running for re-election, Ford narrowly missed defeat when Ronald Reagan defeated him in the North Carolina primary. The same year, before Ford's re-election campaign went down in flames, Cheney and Rumsfeld started assembling the

83 Elisabeth Rosenthal, "Study Puts Iraqi Deaths of Civilians at 100,000," *The New York Times International*
84 *The Prince*, Machiavelli

blueprint for a triumphant hawkish agenda to prolong the Cold War indefinitely. I say indefinitely because, although the Cold War is technically over, these strategies have continued into the present. Nixon spoke out in 1971 about the need to "reduce the level of fear, by reducing the causes of fear." But the hawks in his successor's cabinet wanted the opposite: they loved the way fear shapes public opinion. They wanted the defense budget pumped up, they wanted victory in the "police conflict" of Vietnam, and if they had to invent "new causes of fear" to convince voters, they were willing.

In 1976, the CIA reported that the Soviet Union was decaying from within and would soon fall apart. But Rumsfeld countered with his trademark bureaucratic babble:

"The Soviet Union has been busy. They've been busy in terms of their level of effort; they've been busy in terms of the actual weapons they've been producing; they've been busy in terms of expanding production rates; they've been busy in terms of expanding their institutional capability to produce additional weapons at additional rates; they've been busy in terms of expanding their capability to increasingly improve the sophistication of those weapons."

Just like today, when Cheney and Rumsfeld don't like what the CIA says, they form a rival intelligence group. In 1976, they called it the President's Foreign Intelligence Advisory Board (PFIAB), and eventually issued three reports. The third report was the most controversial, the "Team B Strategic Objectives Panel."

Director of CIA William Colby pleaded with President Ford, against letting the Team B monster see the light of day: "It is hard for me to envisage how an ad hoc 'independent' group of government and non-government analysts could prepare a more thorough, comprehensive assessment of Soviet strategic capabilities...than the intelligence community can prepare."[86] But Colby was soon replaced by a new head of CIA, George H.W. Bush who signed off on the ad hoc group with gusto, "Let her fly!! OK, G.B.," he wrote.[87]

While the CIA was saying that the USSR was falling apart, Team B issued statements and reports that said the Soviet Union was developing sophisticated new weapons systems. For example, they claimed the USSR was developing a new nuclear submarine fleet undetectable by sonar. When asked for proof, Team B said there was none, since the new weapons system was undetectable. "If you go through most of Team B's specific alle-

85 The Power of Nightmares, BBC three-part television series; 2005.
86 William E. Colby to President Ford (Nov. 21, 1975), private collection of Dr. Cahn
87 George A. Carver, Jr., "Note for the Director," May 26, 1976.

The Big Wedding:

gations about weapons systems, and you just examine them, one by one, they were all wrong," federal arms control expert Dr. Anne Cahn told the BBC.[85]

Team B released its report right before the election of 1976, and claimed that the USA was lagging behind the USSR in the arms race. The timing of the release was designed to be a kind of "October Surprise" against Carter, but this one didn't work. Upon taking power, President Carter purged Bush and about eight hundred other suspicious characters (including Ted Shackley) from the CIA. Four years later, a lot of those same characters interfered with the election again by negotiating with Iran to hold onto the hostages a little longer. Team B became the "A Team" when Reagan/Bush/Cheney came to power in 1981.

For twelve years, the country was subjected to a series of new "causes to fear": Muammar Qaddafi, Manuel Noriega, Daniel Ortega and the Sandinistas, the "Communist" government in Afghanistan, etc. These were the straw men, garish bogeymen the government and media propped up, only to knock them down. It was a "Big Lie," but many behind the scenes surely said it was a "noble lie." It justified a military budget out of control, while the White House cut funding for school lunches.

Back to Dr. Cahn:

> "The United States embarked on a trillion dollar defense buildup. As a result, the country neglected its schools, cities, roads and bridges, and health care system...From the world's greatest creditor nation, the United States became the world's greatest debtor—in order to pay for arms to counter the threat of a nation that was collapsing."

Nobody understands it can happen again. Or that it's happening right now.

The GOP hawks despised the restraint President Bush showed in not invading Baghdad. Bush feared an Iraqi quagmire, and stuck with the stated goal of the coalition he had assembled: to expel Iraq from Kuwait. In a rage, Scooter Libby and Team B veteran Paul Wolfowitz wrote the report "Defense Planning Guidance" for then-Defense Secretary Dick Cheney, in 1992. The report called for pre-emptive strikes on countries developing weapons of mass destruction. Those ideas were recycled and reissued in 2000 by the Project for a New American Century (PNAC), under the title, "Rebuilding America's Defenses: Strategies Forces and Resources for a New Century."

The rehash incorporated some ideas from the 1997 book *The Grand Chessboard* by Zbigniew Brzezinski, National Security Advisor to Presidents Carter and Reagan. The point is "to keep the barbarians from coming together," Zbigniew Brzezinski had written in *The Grand Chessboard*. America, scolded Brzezinski, is "fixated on mass entertainment...heavily dominated by hedonistic and socially escapist themes." Since the USA is such an "increasingly multi-cultural society," and the everyday working people are not inclined to support any more Vietnams, the only thing that will motivate massive emotional support for foreign wars is something like "the shock effect of the Japanese attack on Pearl Harbor." America will likely "find it more difficult to fashion a consensus on foreign policy issues, except in the circumstance of a truly massive and widely perceived direct external threat." Likewise, the PNAC manifesto in 2000 recognized the need for a "cataclysmic event of the magnitude of Pearl Harbor."

According to Paul Wolfowitz and Scooter Libby, the invasion of Iraq is just an "immediate justification" for the U.S. to "play a more permanent role in Gulf regional security."

PNAC's defining principles swore to "accept responsibility for America's unique role in preserving and extending an international order friendly to our security, our prosperity, and our principles." In other words, to become the world's policeman who enforces not some kind of higher law, but whatever's clever for American big business.

The PNAC report nakedly demanded huge jumps in U.S. military spending. It demanded military bases in Central Asia and the Middle East, the toppling of non-compliant regimes, the shredding of international treaties, total control of the world's energy resources, militarization of outer space, complete control of the internet, and a willingness to use nuclear weapons to achieve American goals.

Before resuming the post of Secretary of Defense, Rumsfeld wrote a paper of his own, the "Vision for 2020," which argued for a new generation of space weapons "to protect U.S. interests and investment" since "The globalization of the world economy...will continue with a widening between the haves and the have-nots."

Somewhere in this candid language about the naked abyss of the growing class divide, I hear a sublimated cry for justice. The masters of war know what they are doing is wrong. Their humanity is not totally gone. The truth comes out in mysteriously nude language.

When I punched a Nazi skinhead on Capitol Hill in August of 2002, I engaged in political violence for the last time. Shortly afterward, I spent a good deal of time in New Mexico reading Gandhi. When I punched the Nazi, what I really wanted to do was break through to him and break out of this whole cycle of violence. But I realized later that I failed to reach him and instead just tagged the guy in the face. Gandhi says that the oppressor is still human. Somewhere in Rumsfeld's technocratic neo-con heart, he's gotta know he's living in a fantasy land. Imperialism is dead, it is death. To rule by fear and the power of guns and dollars is pure fascism. When I punched that Nazi I wanted to be a revolutionary, but I was only a novice.

The Big Wedding:

CHAPTER 10

MICHAEL CHERTOFF: TERROR'S DEFENDER

When he entered private practice, Chertoff said he would not
represent drug dealers and mobsters, preferring to work for "decent people."

—Bergen County Record, June 19, 2000

In the context of the intersection between the neo-cons and
Muslim Brotherhood, perhaps it's no longer outlandish to
suggest that if you want to get ahead in government today, what
you should do is defend the financiers of Islamic terror in court,
and do your part to support White House cover-ups. That's
exactly what Michael Chertoff did with his life. As a result, his
nomination as Director of Homeland Security was so weird the
Senate was unwilling to deal with it. He was confirmed without
controversey.

Michael Chertoff defended Dr. Magdy Elamir, a financier of
Osama bin Laden, and kept him out of jail. He looked the other
way during the investigation into the death of White House
lawyer Vince Foster. Chertoff advised the White House and CIA
on the legality of torture. He's right at home in an
Administration rocketing the country towards all-out fascism.

THE 9/II MONEY

The June 20, 2000 *Bergen County Record* reported that as a private attorney, Michael Chertoff defended Dr. Magdy Elamir, a suspected terrorist financier. Dr. Elamir's HMO was sued by the State of New Jersey to recoup $16.7 million in losses. At least $5.7 million was unaccounted for, funneled "to unknown parties...by means of wire transfers to bank accounts where the beneficial owner of the account is unknown."[88]

Magdy Elamir financially supported the Al Salam Mosque, where blind Sheikh Omar Abdel-Rahman preached before he was arrested for his role in the 1993 World Trade Center bombing.

This is the same Dr. Magdy Elamir who was featured in the "Dateline NBC" investigation with Randy Glass. In fact, Glass said he had spoken with Dr. Elamir as part of his undercover infiltration of the ISI-linked arms dealers. "Dateline" reported that intelligence reports accused Dr. Elamir of having "had financial ties with Osama bin Laden for years." During a recorded telephone conversation with Glass, Elamir's brother, Mohamed, tried to purchase "small arms and ammunition."

In the words of attorney Lynne Stewart, "even the most despicable deserve representation." But as Stewart knows, unless you have White House connections, defending the despised can carry a high price. Stewart herself faces thirty years for actions taken in defense of the blind Sheikh. Chertoff's client, Dr. Elamir, was a suspect in a highly-monitored, sensitive operation at the center of the secret history of 9/11. But thanks to Michael Chertoff, Elamir was exonerated. Unlike Stewart, Chertoff didn't get 30 years for defending a terrorist. He even got his client off.

"Dateline" reported that Dr. Elamir and his corporations paid at least five thousand dollars to arms dealer Diaa Mohsen. In an ambush interview on camera, Dr. Elamir referred to Mohsen as "a family friend."

"By the time Operation Diamondback culminated in arrests in the summer of 2001, Michael Chertoff was the assistant attorney general in charge of the criminal division, and Operation Diamondback would have fallen under his purview, since it was a criminal case and not a counterterrorism case," said researcher Allan Duncan.

---

88 Elise Young, "State Sues HMO Founder To Recoup Millions," *Record* (Bergen Co., NJ) June 20, 2000

MASTER OF FINANCES

Fresh from his defense of Elamir, in October 2001, Chertoff was picked by the White House to head Operation Green Quest, the multi-agency initiative to target sources of funding for terrorist organizations. Chertoff told the Associated Press on Oct. 25, 2001 that, "The lifeblood of terrorism is money, and if we cut the money we cut the blood supply."

Two years later, former White House terrorism czar Richard Clarke stated, "The U.S. effort to shut down financial support for terrorist networks is being seriously hampered by a government reorganization that has left the most experienced agencies without any real power." Clarke headed counter-terrorism at the White House for the Clinton and Bush administrations before leaving government in 2003. "The decision to put the Federal Bureau of Investigation in charge of terror finance investigations, and to give new powers to the Department of Homeland Security, [has] set the campaign back."[89]

In Congressional testimony, Clarke made comments similar to what Randy Class says in Chapter 11 about the FBI:

> "Having the current structure, where the FBI is in charge and tells everybody else what to do, is a recipe, I think for failure...The FBI by tradition doesn't co-operate well with other federal agencies and it doesn't share information. It treats other federal agencies as second-class participants in the overall effort."

While head of Green Quest, Michael Chertoff played a central role in formulating U.S. anti-terrorism policy, which included a vast expansion of police powers and the secret detention of hundreds of Middle Easterners in the United States.

Chertoff was one of the chief architects of Title III of the USA Patriot Act, also known as the International Money Laundering Abatement and Financial Anti-Terrorism Act of 2001. Chertoff then served as assistant attorney general of the Criminal Division at the Department of Justice from 2001 to 2003 (the post is the same one Robert Mueller held when he stymied Senator John Kerry's investigation into BCCI).

---

89 Edward Alden, "Shake-Up Amid War on Terror 'Has Hit Campaign'" *Financial Times* 23 October 2003; p. 2.

THE VINCE FOSTER CONNECTION

Patrick Knowlton was a licensed DC private investigator. He spent seven years looking into the death of White House attorney Vincent Foster. Having voted for Clinton, he wasn't attracted to the issue out of any anti-Democrat ire. Knowlton happened to stumble into the topic, literally, on July 20, 1993 when he stopped at Fort Marcy Park in Arlington, VA. Something about the scene struck him as odd; he observed a man glaring at him menacingly in the park's parking lot. When Knowlton came out of the woods after relieving himself, the man was still there, still staring.

Knowlton later found out he had been there seventy minutes before Foster's body was discovered. But he learned that none of the cars he saw in the small park's parking lot matched the description for Vince Foster's silver car. Over the next seven years, as Knowlton spoke out, he became a grand jury witness to the Starr inquiry. He faced intense harassment from individuals he discovered were working for the FBI. He filed a lawsuit against FBI Special Agent Russel Bransford and others.

Meanwhile, he observed the bipartisan Senate investigation pursuing a lackadaisical investigation, advised by Senate Counsel Michael Chertoff. "Chertoff knew what we knew," Knowlton told me, "it wasn't that hard to find. Nobody could leave that much information out there unless they knew nobody was going to get to it. And that was Chertoff's job, not to get to it."

"It was obvious Foster's car wasn't in the park, Michael Chertoff never went near that issue," said Patrick Knowlton.

"One of the things he was notorious for is that he would never do follow-up questions."

Knowlton was referencing the time that Chertoff was taking the deposition of park police officer Cheryl Braun. Braun mysteriously mentioned a visit to the hospital morgue "to retrieve some property" on her way from the park to inform Foster's family. Chertoff seemed incurious as to the nature of that strange diversion.

When park police officer John Rolla was under oath with the other incurious Senate Counsel, Richard Ben-Veniste, Rolla blurted out that he didn't find any car keys on Foster's body: "I searched [Foster's] pants pockets. I couldn't find a wallet or nothing in his pants pockets. Later on, Investigator Braun and myself...searched the car and we were puzzled why we found no keys to the car."

Neither Ben-Veniste nor Chertoff seemed interested in asking why Foster's car was not at Fort Marcy Park until after Foster allegedly committed suicide. The attorneys also ignored why, according to police testimony, Foster's car keys weren't on his person when police searched his body in the park.

Knowlton and a group of researchers concluded that Foster did not commit suicide on July 20, 1993. But that conclusion was outside the Washington consensus.

In a surprise twist, the three judges in the U.S. Court of Appeals who supervised Independent Counsel Ken Starr ordered Starr to include a twenty-page addendum to his report on Foster. The addendum, submitted by Knowlton's attorney John H. Clarke, included evidence that Foster was murdered, as well as documentation of the witness intimidation Knowlton had suffered. Legal researcher Hugh Turley, who assisted Knowlton's case, told me, "This addendum marked the first time in U.S. history an independent counsel had criminal activity by his own staff attached to his report!"

I asked John H. Clarke, Knowlton's lead attorney, for his impression of Chertoff: "He's a dishonest bastard. He went along with the Foster cover-up." When Clarke, Turley, and Knowlton tried to get the media to look at the addendum to Starr's report, key members of the Washington press corps told them that the "official story" of suicide had already been determined to be true, and that writing about Knowlton's harassment by FBI would only "raise more questions."

ON THE FAST TRACK

In June 2003, Michael Chertoff was nominated to the Third Circuit U.S. Court of Appeals. Though there is no formal career path for federal judges, it is common for appellate judges to serve as district judges prior to being appointed to a circuit court, according to the Administrative Office of the United States Courts. Despite having never served in the judiciary, Chertoff was made a Judge for the Third Circuit Court of Appeals, whose jurisdiction includes Delaware, New Jersey, Pennsylvania, and the U.S. Virgin Islands.

After nineteen months on the bench of the Third Circuit Court of Appeals, Chertoff was nominated by President Bush to the position of Secretary of Homeland Security.

"It's an exceptional rise to power," quipped Tom Fitton, president of Judicial Watch.

Michael Chertoff advised the CIA on the legality of torture techniques in Afghanistan and at Abu Ghraib prison. His confirmation hearings focused on this; but, by using the spotlight to denounce torture, Chertoff was able to make it a public relations coup. Little time was spent on the fact that Chertoff had personally cut a deal with the lawyers for John Walker Lindh, the "American Taliban," who had been about to testify about his torture at the hands of his jailers in June 2002.[90] Chertoff's deal gagged Lindh and prevented public awareness of U.S. torture until the Abu Graib prison scandal in late April 2004.

Chertoff was approved as Director of Homeland Security. Meanwhile, journalists banged their heads on the wall trying to get editors to look at Chertoff's involvement in Operation Diamondback. For example, around this time, I spoke with John Pacenti at the *Palm Beach Post*, who had originally tipped me off to Chertoff's posting as an Assistant U.S. Attorney, despite his past defending Elamir. As I worked on a piece on Chertoff for the *University Star*,[91] Pacenti complained that he was having trouble getting a story approved on Chertoff/Elamir for the *Post*.

Randy Glass later told me that John Mintz at the *Washington Post* had similar trouble. Mintz and the *Post* share stories with NBC on occasion. The day the "Dateline" story was broadcast, Mintz wrote a front-page preview story on Glass. The story didn't mention Dr. Elamir.

Around the time of Chertoff's confirmation hearings, Glass contacted Mintz. Glass remembers, "John loved it—Chertoff—that whole piece...All of a sudden, John called me up and said, 'Randy, you know, listen. They're not letting me run with it...something funny's going on. I talked to other people in the biz...There's a lot of strings being pulled in town. And everything you told me is true, we verified everything.'"

I phoned Mr. Mintz at the *Post*. He insisted that his comments to me not be quoted. But to paraphrase, he denied that he had said the above to Glass. As his tone became increasingly hostile, Mintz insisted that he had made a decision free from outside influence—the Chertoff/Elamir story didn't meet his criteria for what he could put in the *Washington Post*. He eventually accused me of implying that he had missed a story here, and called the Elamir angle a conspiracy theory.

90 Dave Lindorff, "Chertoff and Torture," Posted 27 January 2005
http://www.thenation.com/doc.mhtml?i=20050214&cs=lindorff
91 The piece appeared in San Marcos University's *University Star* and was co-written with Melissa Johnson. http://www.universitystar.com/main/article.php?aid=1236

Director of CIA William Colby once said the "the Central Intelligence Agency owns everyone of any major significance in the major media." Now, I'm not a fan of broad generalizations. But the Mintz experience didn't help me develop a moderate stance. When Mintz jumped down my throat just for asking a few questions about why he took a pass on the Chertoff/Elamir story, I wasn't all that surprised. Remember, this is the same reporter who, in his *Washington Post* news features, ran stories featuring CIA people expressing how benevolent and useful the Muslim Brotherhood is.

The Big Wedding:

CHAPTER II

FLORIDA NOTEBOOK: RANDY GLASS AND ARNIE KRUITHOFF IN TERRORLAND

©Rick McKay/The Palm Beach Post

Since first meeting Randy Glass over the phone in July of 2004, I interviewed him over ten times for this book. Early on in our relationship he promised to play me the "Frank Taylor tape" once he was off probation, after March 15, 2005. On March 18, my wife Holley Anderson and I were at his front door in Boca Raton with a video camera. We taped fifteen hours of raw footage on the trip. We spent a day and an evening with Glass and then cut across the state to catch up with Hopsicker and the curious characters of Venice.

Randy Glass, in person, is a charmer. He's a former LSD tripper, a vegetarian, and a self-professed child of the '60s. He did six months in the army when he was seventeen and he was honorably discharged for "not being able to adapt to Army life." He qualified to go to college on the GI bill which flew him to

Europe where he started a hash export business. He eventually moved back to Baltimore and opened four car washes. But that life was boring, so he went into various criminal enterprises. He's been married five times, but is single now. He may or may not have $30 million stashed somewhere and would prefer not to talk about it. Today, he drives a black Beemer around Boca and knows everyone. He can walk into a supermarket and say four charming things to four separate women in four minutes. He's Mr. Sunshine in an already very bright place.

The way he tells it, Glass got his first supervising agent at ATF, Pete Liston, taken off the case, right after Glass started there. "I told them it was either him or me, because I'm not getting killed working with that guy." If Glass, an undercover informant, could get his supervising agent axed right at the outset of his collaboration with ATF, then that means that Glass started there with a heavyweight reputation. Maybe Glass's contacts in the Gambino and Gotti families have something to do with that.

Glass's sparsely furnished home is decorated with pictures of himself with Donald Trump and Clint Eastwood. We sat down in a cavernous main room with glossy marble tiles covering the entire floor. His small, hyper, brown poodle, "Peanut," barked at the large birds that waddled up from the lake.

When I asked about the Frank Taylor tape, he was uncomfortable. He said contacts in the National Security Administration had warned him about sharing it twice, and Steve Burdelski from FBI had also said it wouldn't be prudent.

I asked him:

"You're telling me...we can't hear the tapes from summer of 2001 of the State Department guy telling you about planes being flown into the World Trade Center."

"I've got some serious worries about that."

"Do you have worries about talking to us today?"

"Yes of course"

"Do you feel we're being monitored right now?"

"Absolutely. I'm sure that they monitor my phone...there was a time when I would have happily played stuff for you, but there's trouble brewing on the horizon—there's a lot of stuff. I just want to live through it."

However, what Glass was able to share with us was worth the trip. He reflected on a moment in the "Dateline NBC" piece (August 2, 2002) when veteran ATF undercover agent Dick Stoltz said he couldn't believe this operation hadn't been taken over by the FBI or CIA. This time, Glass said, "It was. Dick Stoltz didn't know it." Glass had told him about conversations Stoltz had had with R.G. Abbas. But domestic law enforcement hadn't monitored the call. "How would you know?" asked Stoltz. Glass's contacts in "Spooksville" had been listening in on Stoltz's calls with Abbas. They had overseen the entire ATF sting operation.

"What do you think the NSA does? That's what they do. Listening to everything. Every single fax, every single call."

The way Glass tells it, when Pakistan is there, so are top intelligence operators. In ways the ATF doesn't even dream of, Glass indicated the NSA & CIA were key elements of the "Spooksville" who monitored the story. But when one recalls that BCCI gave Pakistan the ability to download U.S. spy satellite data, one realizes that "NSA & CIA" only begin to describe the powerful secretive organizations at work here.

I asked Glass:

If the NSA is that powerful, and there are reports that Osama bin Laden's satellite phone was monitored on September 10, and you've got State Department telling you, don't worry, we know, then it seems to me that 9/11 was allowed to happen so that we could get into some wars that we wanted to get into.

"That's correct. That's 100 percent correct. 9/11 was supposed to be a nuclear attack."

And instead of stopping it, we just downgraded it?

"Correct. Exactly correct. I was part of an operation to stop the nuclear part of it. Pakistan's ISI was behind 9/11...A.Q. Khan's assistant is who we showed the weapons-grade plutonium to."

If Glass identifies in a vague way with the student politics of the late '60s, why does he occasionally pop off with something straight out of the neo-con handbook? Maybe this is the closest thing to a smoking gun that Glass is indeed communicating with some heavies high up in intel: this political bias that comes out in his observations on foreign policy. For example:

"There are large terrorist cells in Venezuela. Al Qaeda and Hezbollah have cells there."

Glass repeatedly slams Hugo Chavez's social-democratic regime in Venezuela as a hotbed of terrorists. The evidence on this is scant. No media sources, corporate or independent, have reported it, outside of Venezuela itself, where Chavez's opposition owns most of the media.[92] There are two sources trying to advance the theory, but both are embittered defectors.[93]

92 According to the BBC, 60 percent of the Venezuelan TV is owned by just two men, one of which President Chavez refers to as a "fascist." http://news.bbc.co.uk/1/hi/world/americas/3524760.stm
93 While researching this point, I spoke with an Albuquerque investment banker who has advised the Chavez government's Treasury. He had this to say on the Chavez-linked-to-terrorism theory: "The allegations are likely right-wing-instigated for political purposes. They don't have a shred of truth to them."

The Bush White House supported a short-lived coup against Chavez on April 12, 2002. So each time Glass advances strange rumors, President Bush's policy goals blatantly show through his rhetoric on Venezuela.

Glass maintains that the sole culprit for 9/11 at any national level is Pakistan. This position absolves all other culprits, like the international far right, or the Saudi Arabian funding of Muslim Brotherhood and its various manifestations. One of the many tapes Glass played for us is of FBI agent Charlie Wilcox, early in the investigation. In it, Glass made reference to Diaa Mohsen's connection to the Saudi Royal family. But when I asked Glass about this, he was suddenly adamant that Mohsen had nothing to do with the Saudis.

I asked Glass, "Why would the CIA/NSA want to work with a former jewelry con man, then with the ATF?"

Glass laughed bitterly at my naïveté.

> *"Are you kidding? Do you have any idea who these people work with? Who do you think these people are? What do you think that they need? Let's take the FBI. They send a guy to Undercover School. Undercover 101. Who do you think they have? Some college preppy...He's never been out of the country...As opposed to a guy with world skills who's been out conning international businessmen his whole life?*

"Did you find your skill set from the past helped you in your work here?"

> *"I felt right at home. Of course!"*

Glass's diamond-broker past was an asset when he was a "double agent" in a job involving diamonds-for-guns in the Democratic Republic of Congo.

"What can you tell us about your background in the diamond industry?"

On this one, his voice goes low, almost a whisper, as if to say, now, at last, we're talking about some sensitive material...

> *"Everybody's a gypsy. And anyone that says that they aren't is lying...The intelligence guys make somebody like me look like a little kid. Because they got the juice, understand? They've got the authority, they can do anything, they can make magic happen, they don't even have to flash their credentials. They're all connected, they are wired."*

Several times during our talk, I noticed that the way that Glass used the term "double agent" to describe himself was odd. He hadn't been a spy working for both sides in an operation. But because of his veneer of criminality, he was dangled in front of foreign intelligence, so that they would try and get him to betray the U.S. He was a tool—a method of finding out which foreign nationals were recruiters for foreign intelligence. For instance, Glass relates how he visited the Egyptian Embassy—and they took the bait. They made him an offer and tried to recruit him as a double agent. U.S. intelligence learned something that day.

I got the impression that Glass's compelling likeability, his street cred, and his freelance status had won the confidence of higher-ups in Spooksville. Glass claims they told him stuff they couldn't tell the ATF or FBI. That's good, because his experiences at the FBI had left a lot to be desired.

"Dave Frasca was head of the West Palm Beach Terrorism Task Force," Glass constantly reminded me. At the beginning, Frasca was reluctant to approve funds and open an investigation regarding Mohsen. According to the Chuck Wilcox tape, Frasca told Wilcox, "This guy is talking about this, to this, to this, it's like a movie script...it sounds too good to be true."

Glass remembers: "[Steve] Barborini jumped in [Frasca's] face and said, 'Hey, you let $15 thousand walk for a kilo of cocaine...this guy is talking about sophisticated weapons systems, bin Laden...heroin and rocket-propelled grenades. Glass is going to pay for his passport up front. And you're telling me you're not going to open a case?' And he said no. So, Barborini came to me and said 'Fuck him.' That's when he went to U.S. Customs, because ATF doesn't have the budget. I ended up financing the case. They are the FBI; their job is to investigate. Not to think, well, you know, sounds too good to be true...."

Steve Barborini's stand against the more powerful FBI is a commendable move, and maybe there's a lesson here. It seems the more centralized, powerful, insular, non-transparent an organization is, the more corrupt it becomes. Maybe instead of one big central domestic intelligence group, the government needs to hire a gigantic consulting firm to advise how to implement more transparency, cooperation, and oversight.

Glass bought his Venezuelan passport from Diaa Mohsen for $12 thousand, and had to put up $6 thousand of his own money to do it. Wilcox warned Glass that the FBI might stick him with the other half of the bill.

On tape, Charlie Wilcox, FBI, is eerily similar to John Anticev of the FBI when he complained about expense reports to Emad Salem(see Chapter 4). Charlie Wilcox complained, "I don't even trust my own agency sometimes—they'll tell me they're going to do something and then they'll just armchair it for a couple days, and then they'll say we're not going to do that, and then after I've told you to do it, they'll say, well, we never really signed or authorized you to do that."

Glass's lasting impressions of the FBI?

> *"I have no respect for the FBI, at all, under any circumstances. They are inept, they do not cooperate with other agencies, they are bullies, they are control freaks, they threaten people. They charge people for things that they don't deserve. They get away with it, because people don't believe they would do anything like that."*

A recent "critical history" of the FBI argues that Glass is right. The FBI's behavior at Waco, Ruby Ridge, and the Atlanta Olympics bombing "suggested that an insular culture of secrecy shaped how FBI officials responded whenever FBI operations became subjected to critical scrutiny."[94]

"When's the last time you heard about an FBI agent getting fired?" asked Randy.

The USA badly needs a reform of its secret police. With the FBI's history, everywhere you turn, ugly facts pop up. One week before Timothy McVeigh's execution, four thousand papers in his FBI file still had not been turned over to the defense.[95] The Senate Judiciary Committee had major critical hearings scheduled on the FBI...from June to September 2001. 9/11 scuttled that plan, and the hearings were never concluded. But before 9/11, Senator Patrick Leahy called the FBI "unmanageable, unaccountable, and unreliable. Its much vaunted independence has been transformed for some into an image of insular arrogance."[96]

Glass isn't the only public critic of David Frasca. Author Michael Ruppert levied the most serious charges against Frasca in his authoritative 674-page opus *Crossing the Rubicon.*[97] Ruppert linked him to five major incidents of whistle-blower suppression and cover-up associated with 9/11. In three of the five cases, the whistle-blowers were FBI agents who spoke up and experienced severe backlash. Each of the three had access to information that could have prevented the 9/11 attack.

Coleen Rowley, who publicly chastised FBI director Robert Mueller in 2002, said in our interview, "I've been flabbergasted by actually more than just Frasca, to the point where I've stopped being surprised at it." The problem is a reverse meritocracy. There's no systemic incentive to coming to work at FBI headquarters, "People in the FBI just hate working in Washington, D.C. and all the disincentives that, to commuting and all these other things...so the people who have the most blinding ambition, not necessarily competency, are the ones that

94 Althan Theoharris. *The FBI and American Democracy: A Brief Critical History.* (University Press of Kansas, 2004) this little book is an admirable start, but it only scrapes the surface of the problem. There's no acknowledgement of Professor Ward Churchill's breakthrough research on FBI COIN-TELPRO; 9/11 is lightly touched upon with no mention of David Frasca. Iran/Contra Investigator Richard Taus's FBI railroading is ignored.
95 ibid.
96 ibid.
97 Michael C. Ruppert, *Crossing the Rubicon: The Decline of the American Empire at the End of the Age of Oil* (Canada: New Society Publishers, 2004)

tend to raise their hand and then go up the ladder. They don't have incentives pay-wise or other reasons enough...so many of our best agents stay in the agent role rather than raising their hand and going up."

Recall also that David Frasca's interference was the subject of protest from FBI Special Agents Robert Wright and Ken Williams. Wright was with the FBI's Chicago division, who tracked bin Laden's finances. However, one year after 9/11, he gave an explosive, emotional press conference in which he said that his superiors had stopped him from preventing 9/11.[98] Ken Williams, in the Arizona field office, wrote the "Phoenix Memo" requesting an investigation into terrorists at U.S. Flight Schools. Frasca read it and quashed it.

Ruppert builds an argument toward a conclusion that Frasca "was the primary agent responsible for the deliberate, willful, and arguably harmful suppression of evidence and of investigations that could well have prevented 9/11." Citing work by government researchers, Ruppert makes the case that Frasca may well be working for somebody else, like CIA. In *Rubicon,* Ruppert writes "The role he played before 9/11 clearly served interests other than those of the FBI, or the innocent Americans killed or bereaved by the attacks."

Coleen Rowley has seen Ruppert's speeches, and is aware of his conclusions about Frasca. She doesn't subscribe to the theory, but she did point out to me that Frasca's boss, Michael Rollins, is equally as culpable.

Did the FBI know the date and the city of the 9/11 attack in advance? In Florida in 2005, Glass now stated they did. He also claimed that he did.

> *"I knew the day and the city. And I was in jail. I knew EVERYTHING. I couldn't stand it; I couldn't live with it. I knew I was going to jail. I couldn't fucking do anything. If I went to the fucking law enforcement guys, nothing could happen, they'd be shut down immediately and I'd probably be killed."*

"How did you know about 9/11?"

> *"The spooks, they knew. OK? First, the State Department guys told me. Then, I called my spook guys. I said, 'listen, I'm about to fucking go public. I haven't discussed this with anyone. Now that I have the threats, I am not going to do anything about it'."*

Glass turns his head and shouts at the ceiling:

> *"Got it? Of course we knew. First, the State Department told me, then the FBI."*

---

98 See original Judicial Watch press release at http://www.judicialwatch.org/printer_2469.shtml "FBI Agent Robert Wright Says FBI Agents Assigned to Intelliengence Operations Continue to Protect Terrorists from Criminal Investigations and Prosecutions"

When Glass got sentenced to seven months for fraud, it was only thanks to the zeal of prosecutor Neil Karadbil. The FBI and ATF agents wanted Glass fully acquitted for his work as an informant, and when Glass got seven months, Steve Burdelski threw Neil Karadbil against the wall, out in the hall, after the sentencing. The sentence wrecked Glass's fifth marriage.

But Spooksville forgives. They told Glass to go do his time, and that he could come back to work for them when he was out. He worked for them right upon release, during his probation—which is technically illegal, but in this case, with a snap of the fingers, technicalities were handled.

After 9/11, Glass was moved to a lockdown facility. "They weren't sure what to do with me. They knew what I had. They moved me from camp to a lockdown facility, and I couldn't speak to any of the [intelligence] guys, but I did speak to the local guys, and I actually thought I was gonna get killed."

Glass dug around for the videotapes of the Senator Bob Graham interview. While he went from room to room throwing around battered suitcases full of tapes, Glass provided new insights into why the Senator Bob Graham/WPTV interview actually took place that day in September 2002.

> *"I called his Chief of Staff [Charlie Yonts] and told him unless Bob Graham told the truth, because I was sick and tired of him lying to the American people about his bullshit investigation, the joint Congressional/Senate investigation, unless he told the truth. At that news conference, I was going to go public with the tapes that I had."*
>
> *"And, his Chief of Staff said, 'Randy, you keep telling us you have these tapes, and I've never heard them. So why should we believe that you have them?'"*
>
> *"I told him to put his fucking ear a little closer to the phone, and pushed the button."*

"What was on those tapes?"

> *"What do you think was on those tapes?"*

"Bob Graham?"

> *"Of course. I did have a meeting with him; it wasn't just with Charlie Yonts. And I told him [Graham] specifically, specifically, the information I had about airplanes flying into the World Trade Center."*

"When did you meet with Bob Graham?"

> *"Around July 2001."*

Glass pulls out a videotape. It's the raw, unedited tape of the Senator Graham interview from September 22, 2002, on

WPTV NBC, West Palm Beach. We grab a seat on the leather couch.

Kathleen Walters asked, "How serious was the threat from Randy Glass?"

The senator gave a long-winded non-answer all about the procedures of intelligence routing.

On tape, Senator Graham claimed he "did not know the specifics" of the information Glass provided. This is pretty easy to disprove, using Graham's own statements. Graham said: "I have no reason to believe Mr. Glass's piece of information was not treated appropriately." But when the reporter Kathleen Walters pressed the senator, pointing out that it got no response, Graham retorted, "I could give you a number of examples of information that was analogous to what Mr. Glass said."

Hey wait, Bob, if you "did not know the specifics" of Mr. Glass's information, how could you know what was "analogous" to it?

RANDY AT THE JOINT INQUIRY

According to the *Palm Beach Post*, "Glass spent 3 1/2 hours under oath" on Oct. 16, 2002 at the Senate/House Joint Inquiry. That would be about one month after Bob Graham's awkward appearance on WPTV. It seems like Senator Graham, head of Senate Foreign Intelligence, wanted to reel Glass in a little. Glass wasn't exactly a high-profile witness to the Inquiry; he's not on the official witness list in the Joint Inquiry records. His hearing date is not even in the published index of (mostly) closed hearings.

Before testifying, Glass was screened by Rick Cinquegrana, "Deputy Director" of the Joint Inquiry, and by Kay Holt, of the DOJ's Inspector General's office. Cinquegrana was the Joint Inquiry's number two man, under Director Eleanor Hill.[99] The way Glass tells it, he told the two screeners he had evidence and tapes. They told him they were aware of that. They asked him what his intentions were. He said that if keeping secrets would be best for the country, he was willing. He was a team player. But he asked them a question: Are you interested in the Joint Commission hearing the truth? They didn't answer. He had to ask again.

Glass walked into a sealed room in the Rayburn House Office Building. He testified before eighteen to twenty senators and members of Congress. He was going in without his attor-

99 Holt and Cinquegrana both have connections to the CIA, according to Glass and "high-ranking CIA officials."

ney on this one.

"It was very formal. They started to ask me questions. At the beginning, I was very polite. And they began to play little games, and danced around the issue. They did not want to hear direct testimony, or the truth. And finally, I just cut to the chase. And one of them said, 'Excuse me. You, sir, will show respect for this body.'

"I said, 'Listen. Go fuck yourself.'"

To a Congressman?

"To all of them. You know? Fuck them."

Glass said to Congress, "Look, I know I'm a convicted felon. I came in this room to show respect to decent human beings because I thought that you guys were going to show me respect and be decent human beings. But you know? None of you are here to hear the truth, OK? All of you are here to watch over the truth. Because your boss is on a hot seat because there was a news report, and you know if I go public with it, it will bury him. So let's cut the bullshit, and get down to it. Do you want to hear it, or do you just want it to go away?"

They said, "Well first of all, sir, I suggest you watch your language in here."

"Look, I don't need a lesson in manners. And you guys certainly didn't get elected by being Mr. Nice Guy, OK? There's no cameras in here...so let's cut the bullshit."

Later Glass told me, "Of course I recorded it. You think anyone's going to believe me? I know how to protect myself." Glass described a special little device about three to four inches long, designed to be placed in a person's rectum and record conversation from where the sun don't shine. "It costs three hundred dollars and it runs for ten hours. It's digital."

"You actually had it up your ass?"

"Yeah. You're damn skippy. When I had to get up to go to the bathroom, I took it out from the plastic baggy, and I stuck it up my ass. It's digital."

Glass continued: "So anyway, so I sat there and told them, 'I'm not interested in getting anyone into trouble—not interested in attacking anyone, OK? Maybe there's actually a few of you guys here who don't know what's going on. Maybe most of you don't know but I'm here to tell you, OK, so you'll know. And even after, you know, you may not want the truth to come out...because of your boss (and I didn't mean Bob Graham, I meant President Bush). Let's cut to the chase, guys. I know what the game is. I know you want your asses in those seats for the next however many years. I'm not politically stupid. I'm not that smart, I only finished 9th grade, but I think I'm a little smarter than the average bear'."

Then Randy played them some tapes.

"They heard their boss's [Graham's] voice, you know, and the guy who works for their boss [Yonts], they were just like, gone. I said, 'you guys do what you want. I came. I told you—you do what you want, OK? I'm not here to tear the country apart. Let's see what you do with it. Let's see if any one of you has the guts to stand up'.

"Not one of them did."

What had you told them, that you were asking them to act on?

"The truth!"

About?

"That we knew. 'Let 9/11 happen.' We knew, and we kept quiet about it for a larger purpose. I was probably committing suicide. Had I gone public with it, I would have been committing suicide...and they probably knew, if they went public with it, they'd be committing suicide, at least politically. They know."

While we traveled through Florida, I was simultaneously traveling through Florida's history as a staging ground for state terror. I was reading *The War That Never Was*, a 1976 black ops memoir by veteran Bradley Ayers.[100] Ayers had been a decorated captain, plucked from the Army Rangers in the early '60s to train Cuban militias to attack their homeland. He targeted oil refineries and led speed boat convoy search and destroy missions into Cuba. The operation was reporting directly to then-Attorney General Robert F. Kennedy, and the Kennedy White House. When JFK was taken out in Dallas, Ayers realized that he had rubbed elbows with two men widely suspected of being involved in the sniper hit: David Morales and Orlando Bosch. Ayers' boss, JM/Wave Chief of Station Ted Shackley, later went on to various black operations in Laos, Vietnam, and Berlin, before being purged from CIA by Carter in 1977. When Ayers tried to publish all this in '76, his publisher only allowed a censored version.[101]

Reading Ayers' book while in Florida was like penetrating two CIA operations at once, past and present. Two Floridas, overlaid on top of each other. Everywhere we drove, the hurricanes had damaged roofs. New roofs were being put on. The past and present were one. The sun bleached out the color of an over-developed landscape. Yet new construction was happening all the time.

100 Bradley Earl Ayers, *The War That Never Was: An Insider's Account of CIA Covert Operations Against Cuba* (New York: The Bobbs-Merrill Company, Inc., 1976)
101 Vox Pop is republishing the uncensored version in Fall 05, under the title *The Zenith Secret*

In the '80s, Ayers once had told a Florida Court that, during his second career as an undercover DEA agent, he had

> *"entered the secured compounds of Southern Air Transport and Pan Aviation at Miami International Airport on three and four separate occasions, respectively, during the summer and fall of 1985 and the early months of 1986, and on two of the occasions with Southern Air and on three occasions with Pan Aviation, entered aircraft parked on their ramps, collected, examined and tested residue found in the aircraft. I found residue of marijuana and a powdery substance which tested positively as nearly pure cocaine."*

The defense in Southern Air Transport vs. WPLG-TV (ABC-Miami) used Ayers' affidavit in an attempt to prove that both Southern Air and the Pan Aviation airlines "were proprietary interests of the U.S. CIA."[102] As a result, Southern Air Transport was shut down.

I recently asked Ayers whether he had had any funny experiences at the Venice Municipal airport while at DEA.

> *"When things started to heat up in Miami, in Key West, more and more the agency shifted operations, particularly air operations, over onto the West Coast, and Venice was a hot spot, simply because it was so easy to operate out of."*

"You also said you had experience with Arrow Aviation being a CIA proprietary out of Miami?"

> *"Arrow, absolutely...George Bush headed the South Florida Task Force. George Bush, there was no question, was witting all of this activity and I believe that he was placed in charge of the South Florida Task Force because of his involvement in all of these illegal activities...He was the Vice President at that time under Reagan...It was necessary in order to carry on this activity to put somebody down there who had the power, the clout, the stature, to essentially run the operation."*

"So, we're talking about Iran/Contra here, we're talking about Florida being used..."

> *"Go ahead, you're right on track...."*

"Florida effectively being used as one of many places to bring in cocaine from Honduras, related to Iran/Contra and all the black ops cash flow that was going on around Iran/Contra."

> *"You're 100 percent correct, and there were sizable drug smuggling entities operating out of south Florida, some of which I penetrated and reported to my superiors. I, in fact, wore a body bug and was wired and presented specific, hard information where there was no prosecution, there was no follow up. That's the essence of what we're going to talk about in Out of Pocket."*[103]

---

102   Southern Air Transport vs. WPLG-TV (ABC Miami), Case# 87-23989 (11th Cir) See http://www.wethepeople.la /ayers.htm
103   Out of Pocket: Rotten Deals is Brad Ayers's book, planned for 2006.

We arrived in Venice, and Daniel Hopsicker gave us the grand tour. Venice is a pretty town, not flashy, a good town for walking around, a few cafés. There was one good bookstore. Two nice old ladies were running the place. They had *Welcome to Terrorland* displayed right next to the register. It turns out they were big fans of Hopsicker's, and had had some successful book signings with him.

We found Hopsicker in his bungalow, and he took us to Sharky's, the big bar on the beach, where Mohamed Atta was dropped off with Rudi Dekkers right before 9/11. I felt I was not only in *Terrorland,* I was now a character in Hopsicker's book.

We went over to the airport the next day. Huffman Aviation had packed up and left town but their blue awning was still up outside their old building. I walked two doors down into the Florida Flight Training Center building, to see if Arnie Kruithof was still around. Arnie is a flight school owner, a Dutch citizen, and the trainer of 9/11 hijacker Ziad Al-Jarrah.

His front desk lady said, "No, he isn't available, he's in the flight simulator with a customer, who are you with? That camera's not on, is it?"

We made small talk and met a young Austrian flight student named Oliver Drobnik. We took him outside to talk. He told us Arnie is "very internationally connected" and that he "used to fly to South America a lot." We made a note of that.

We took the soft approach with the front desk lady and were very friendly while quietly taping as much as we could. We waited around until Arnie was free. He sat down with us for almost two hours. One of Arnie's first questions for us was whether or not we knew Daniel Hopsicker. I said, "I know him, but I know he's not well-liked in the Venice Police Department or at the local newspaper." Arnie told us that Hopsicker had ambushed him with a camera, antagonistic and full of vitriol, demanding that Arnie "tell him the truth." Arnie had thrown him out.

We took the cue. We kept smiling; we were getting somewhere. Kruithof looks nothing like the photo of him Daniel put on the back cover of *Welcome to Terrorland.* He's about 6'5" with massive biceps and forearms. He's soft-spoken and sun-tanned. He wanted nothing to do with Rudi Dekkers. Arnie had broad anti-war sentiments and remarked, "there are God Bless America stickers everywhere on cars, what about the rest of the world?"

The evidence is strong that Arnie's "international connections" included intelligence. According to Hopsicker, Arnie had received some sort of military training in Missouri. He was reluctant to talk about Florida West, the air service he piloted in South America for a number of years. Was it a passenger line or a cargo line? Arnie wouldn't say until I asked a third time. Finally it came out—cargo, he said, looking down. When the camera was off, Arnie told us he spent a year in a Moroccan jail, but the story there he kept vague.

On June 26, 2002, Kruithof had a near-fatal plane crash. On the heels of Rudi Dekkers' near-fatal helicopter crash, he began to worry that "intelligence" was trying to take him out.

I asked Arnie whom he suspected—U.S. intelligence? He said no; they all blend into each other on the international level-U.S., French, U.K. But if he was just the flight instructor to a certain Lebanese national—why would international intelligence be trying to take him out?

Speaking of blending together, our camera happened to pick up a little detail on the wall when it strayed over the office. A post-it with "Vision Air" written on it next to all the phone numbers. Hmmm. That could have some relation to "VisionAire" a company owned by Wally Hilliard, former owner of Huffman Aviation, and Rudi Dekkers's old boss. And Arnie had just said he had nothing to do with Hilliard.

And what about Florida West? Why was Arnie reluctant to talk about it?

After some digging, we found a few clues: Florida West has been incorporated in a couple of different states at different times, and has been in and out of bankruptcy court. The name Florida West was given in 1984 to a company that up to then had been called...Pan Aero International. Sounds a lot like "Pan Aviation." Or "Aero Systems, Inc." a CIA proprietary company listed in Peter Brewton's *The Mafia, CIA and George Bush*. Brewton listed airlines used to illegally ship arms and military spare parts to Iran and to the Contras.

A website that tracks sales of DC-8 aircraft cited Pan Aero International as a buyer.[104] Those were the planes Arnie said he flew for Florida West.

Later, on the phone, I told Daniel what a favorable impression Kruithof had made. Hopsicker screamed back on the phone, "Who the fuck cares what you think? Arnie was indubitably a part of a U.S. intelligence operation."

If that's true, how much does Arnie actually know about this operation? Now that I understand compartmentalization, I understand that whether 9/11 was Al Qaeda or CIA/Al Qaeda, Arnie was just a stepping-stone. When you're part of an operation, you only know your own part; you don't know the whole pic-

---

104 http://www.dc-8jet.com/na1-dc8-fleet-info.htm

ture, only your compartment.

Some of the strongest moments came when he asked me what my agenda was. He wanted me to level with him. I was happy to oblige. When I told him my 9/11 thesis he developed a look in his eyes of vertigo—this from a pilot. It looked as though similar thoughts had occurred to him. Possibly he was beginning to see the whole show he had played a bit part in.

As we got back on the road to New York, I thought of something Daniel Hopsicker had said, "I just want to be able to pick up a newspaper and read the news."

What Daniel's three years and our five days in Florida proved is that it's not all that difficult to go to the crime scene, explore, and discover. It's surprising there aren't more independent investigators interested in the topic, given the history of Florida and intelligence operations.

Hopsicker, as a result, wants the newspapers to do their job. I'll go him one further and say, if they are not doing their jobs, there must be a reason.

Venice, Florida, and Randy Glass in Boca are rich sources of information about 9/11. These sources contradict an official story with a lot of political power behind it.

If the newspapers reported the news about Florida, they would effectively be putting themselves on the underdog side of an information war.

Their cowardly ducking the story isn't a huge surprise.

CHAPTER 12

A CALL FOR REVOLUTION AND SATYAGRAHA

"These are revolutionary times. All over the globe men are revolting against old systems of exploitation and oppression and out of the wombs of a frail world, new systems of justice and equality are being born. The shirtless and barefoot people of the land are rising up as never before. The people who sat in darkness have seen a great light. We in the West must support these revolutions. It is a sad fact that, because of comfort, complacency, a morbid fear of Communism, and our proneness to adjust to injustice, the Western nations that initiated so much of the revolutionary spirit of the modern world have now become the arch anti-revolutionaries."

—Reverend Dr. Martin Luther King, Jr.,
"Beyond Vietnam"
1967 Speech at Riverside Church

"I never would have agreed to the formulation of the Central Intelligence Agency back in '47, if I had known it would become the American Gestapo."

—President Harry S. Truman

From the witnesses in this book, it's increasingly clear that 9/11 was allowed to happen. 9/11 shows a pathetic desperation on the part of the powerful. They must know their system is in deep crisis. Their status quo global capitalist orgy is losing legitimacy. The extreme nationalism and mass approval for war that 9/11 ushered in is the last resort of a class of rulers determined to divert the power of the people away from our own self-emancipation.

But let's not delay the inevitable: It is time for revolution. It's time to get together on a vision of what the world can be. And a part of that is realizing that others came before us were killed because their vision was so beautiful and powerful it really put the fear of God into the snakes.

Martin Luther King Jr. showed how quickly things can change when we use what we learn from Gandhi: Satyagraha. The word means truth-force, or soul-force. Gandhi's revelation was that not only is it true that God is Truth, but that Truth is God. (This might help those of us who aren't religious per se, or have had bad experiences with religion: we're not talking about dogma, here. We're talking about the truth.) We're talking about bringing the truth back into the picture. It's time.

People all across the political and religious spectrum agree: we don't need any more violence. That's pretty obvious. At the heart of the Arabic word for God, Allah, and the ancient Hebrew word for God, Elohim, is the same root: "El" or "Al," which means One, or "One-ness." It's almost as if at the root of the meaning of "God" is a call to bring people together, to see God in each other, to nurture the Truth that's in each of us. We are built for love. The truth is in our DNA. We were made to speak truth, to execute truthful actions. We all made a promise to the truth a long time ago. It's time to return to that promise.

Historically, the values of the far right, i.e. fascism, have been used by the fat cats of big business as a distraction when their system goes into crisis. Racism is one of their tools to keep workers from even thinking about forming unions together. But since Dr. King, people can see through racism. They quickly saw how effective non-violent social protest was. There became a need for more intense fear-inducing experiences like 9/11. The event and the wars it inspired were a gross distraction from what the people of America and Earth are really capable of: peace, communication, and understanding.

The powermongers of the USA know that when everyday people unite and decide to clean house, in the name of some real democracy, their whole corrupt, racist charade will be over. On that day, their black operations, their secrets, and their back stabbing intelligence networks will be turned over and exposed, like turtles flipped over.

Thanks to the Internet, travel, media, and other new communication technologies, the entire international population has the opportunity to realize an inherent sense of commonality. This new unity will inevitably be the basis for a new era of peace, mutual aid, prosperity, and the equal administration of justice. But since things have been going that way since the late '60s, there's been more intense resistance from the class of people who currently have their hands on the serious mega-capital right now.

The massacre of working people on 9/11 happened because

even "the State" as we know it is in crisis. Because mega-capital is so powerful, the State writhes in a crisis of legitimacy. In my interview with professor and author Dr. Peter Dale Scott, we looked at the evolving definition of the State in a post-9/11 world:

> "What I was taught in political science about the State doesn't apply to what we've got here now. The increasingly overt tyranny is a symptom. The States are not getting stronger. They're getting weaker. They're desperate, and amorphous...I used to call myself an anarchist at one point—but very much a non-violent one."

The question becomes then—how do the masses of people free themselves from the pain of a State in crisis, without resorting to slaughter? The United States government decided some time ago that Lincoln's vision of "government of the people, by the people, for the people" would have to be shoved aside for a State that served mega-capital. Mega-capital loves war because war puts a lock on markets. The United States war machine is a $400 billion a year black hole dedicated to death.[105] It sucks down half the tax dollar of every working American. 9/11 proved that when the U.S. War State runs out of enemies to fear and fight, it creates them.

Even *The 9/11 Commission Report* states: "The U.S. government must define what the message is, what it stands for." It's a moment of rare honesty. And it's also terrifying that these grown-ups got to be so powerful and still they don't know what the U.S. government "stands for."[106]

They lack the courage to say it plain: the USA came of age after World War II on the national stage as a super-power. We could have defined ourselves as a moral leader, an innovator, a noble teacher and elevator of other peoples. Instead, we sacrificed our foundational principles for pure power. The USA is like a bully who happens to be the biggest kid in class, but because he's so scared, he terrifies the other kids.

I have a faith that this life out of balance will in time create a mass movement to correct the problem. We are a great people, America, and the Earth as a whole. As America diversifies ethnically, it becomes more representative of the ethnic diversity of the Earth. We can unite around a set of values that are stronger than the emptiness, confusion, and violence currently being offered. In a world of increasing diversity, bringing people together to talk in a room is the only way to stop the suspicion and betrayal.

The "Big Wedding" was a code word for 9/11 used by some of the terrorists. But 9/11 could actually be a big wedding, between

105   The Department of Defense got $401.3 billion for fiscal 2004, but as Robert Higgs pointed out in the *San Francisco Chronicle*, the total spent on defense is $596.1 billion, when all government spending on defense and "security" is accounted for. ("The Defense Budget Is Bigger Than You Think", *San Francisco Chronicle*, January 18, 2004). The proposed fiscal 2006 defense budget was $419.3 billion.

106   The National Commission on Terrorist Attacks Upon the United States, *The 9/11 Commission Report* (New York: W.W. Norton & Company, 2004) page 376

reality and the future, between a time of deceit and a time of truth, a time of permanent war, and the time for war to end permanently.

OK, but what are the practical steps? Well, for starters, I'd love to see all the ex-whistle-blowers together in one room. Let's throw a conference: The People's Intelligence Network. The P.I.N. to burst this bubble over reality. Let's hold yearly conferences, and tackle topics like narcotics-trafficking, "false-flag" operations, and the creation of "enemies," all of which have become common practices of the U.S. intelligence establishment. Let's start with 9/11. Let's make recommendations and see if we can get someone in power to pay attention. And if we can't, then we'll have to make Satyagraha into a political platform and run some candidates.

The revolution must be electable. The people have had it with self-appointed vanguards on the left or right. I can see a new political movement, based on life, abundant life. Something dedicated to the voice of the people. Something that actually respects the common wisdom, and is willing to put in place a technology and a procedure that listens to it closely.

We will offer life to a people getting sick of all the death. And no matter what happens, no matter what the outcome will be, the struggle itself is meaningful, the challenge is itself invigorating. Let's rock!

APPENDIX I

RICHARD TAUS'S
LETTER TO JOHN ASHCROFT

Richard Taus, 91A1040, LH
Clinton Correctional Facility
P.O. Box 2001
Dannemora, New York 12929

October 15, 2001

Honorable John Ashcroft
Attorney General of the United States
Department of Justice
10th Street, NW & Constitution Ave.
Washington, DC 20530

RE: Anti-Terrorist Information

Dear Mr. Ashcroft:

I was a former FBI Special Agent assigned to the FBINYO (FBI New York Field Office) from 1978 to 1988. I worked on both the Criminal Division and the Foreign Counter-Intelligence Division. My credential number was 3437 and my badge number was 790.

On Friday, October 12, 2001, I was interviewed by two FBI Special Agents (Longerhan and Weissheist (SP?) from the Plattsburgh FBI Resident Agency [RA]) concerning terrorist information disclosed to me from a reliable and credible source. While incarcerated here at Clinton C.F., I became friendly with an individual (source) who has information regarding the participants involved in the tragedies of September 11 and terrorist organizations. It is my opinion that the two interviewing FBI Special Agents failed to conduct a proper and thorough interview, reflecting a "culture" of lethargy as we have seen in past FBI investigations.

The information originally supplied to me on the afternoon of September 11, 2001 by MIAN FAROOQ, New York State DIN Number 00A6040, was accurate and reliable. Subsequent revelations by the news media confirmed FAROOQ's information, that one of the pilots was MOHAMED ATTA. As a result, I pressed him for additional information after discovering the truthfulness of his initial statements.

It is my belief that FAROOQ's information comes from his former contacts with the CIA and his own Pakistani background. (FAROOQ claimed to have been a Pakistani Air Force pilot who flew United Nation missions.) He said he worked for U.S. Customs as an agent at JFK International Airport in New York City. In 1996, FAROOQ stated he met ATTA again at the airport. ATTA was wearing the uniform of an airline pilot. ATTA explained to FAROOQ that his uniform appearance was due to his ownership in a Florida-based flight school. FAROOQ further noted that ATTA became increasingly hostile towards the United States, particularly after ATTA's divorce from his American wife of German/Irish descent. The couple had 3 children.

On October 1, 2001, FAROOQ informed me that he wanted to tell me additional details so that I could supply that information "to the right authority, the FBI." He further noted that he did not trust the CIA and/or his former intelligence handlers, and that he wanted to help the legitimate law enforcement authorities. The additional information is enclosed herein and was provided to the two FBI SAs from the Plattsburgh RA.

I feel that no further action has been taken by the Plattsburgh FBI SAs since FAROOQ notified me that he has not been interviewed by them. Nor did the FBI SAs probe me, during my interview, asking pertinent questions concerning FAROOQ's knowledge and background. Rather, it is my opinion, that the FBI SAs sought only to "RUC" (returned upon completion) close this lead.

With great respect to you, Mr. Ashcroft, the FBI has developed a "culture" which sadly interferes with their investigative mandates. I would go into greater depth about this culture since I was an FBI agent; however, this letter is being directed to you for the sole purpose of further ascertaining and developing information from MIAN FAROOQ whom I believe can contribute to the efforts of the Anti-Terrorism Task Force with his own knowledge and expertise in Pakistani and Afghanistani affairs. The reason I have so diligently pursued this source is to hopefully assist your efforts in preventing any future disasters involving innocent lives.

I have done my best to relay this information to the FBI. In addition to informing New York State Department of

The Big Wedding:

Correctional Services officials, I have reached out to a retired New York City Police Department Captain who notified both the FBINYO and the Melville RA offices on September 18, 22 and October 1 and 4. I also wrote two letters to the ADIC, FBINYO and the Anti-Terrorism Task Force. I pray that you will carefully review this information and have FBI Anti-Terrorism Task Force Special Agents, who are qualified interview Mr. FAROOQ as soon as possible.

Sincerely yours,

Richard Taus

P.S.

October 17, 2001

Later, FAROOQ informed me that he was interviewed by "his" CIA agent and told not to reveal any further information on the above matter. (It could not be ascertained whether FAROOQ was interviewed here or spoke by phone to his former handler.) As a result, FAROOQ would not provide any further information on an alleged doctor who is a bio-chemist. During the first interview/disclosures by FAROOQ on September 11, he mentioned the word "AMTRAK." It was noted, during the October 12 interview with the Plattsburgh RA FBI agents, that FAROOQ occasionally mispronounces words. His reference to "AMTRAK", as the next terrorist threat, could have been a mispronunciation of the word "ANTHRAX."

Based upon my past experiences as an FBI Special Agent, I can only assume that the CIA has a disgruntled former source/asset here whom wants to gain his freedom. Since CIA has done little for him to achieve that end, FAROOQ has tried to approach the FBI through me. My sole purpose in writing this letter is to assist the Joint Anti-Terrorism Task Force with its investigation and prevention of terrorist activities. I seek no benefit or reward. Regrettably from what I have observed, there still appears to be friction between the CIA and FBI in their investigative efforts.

ENCLS: "Confidential Source" (2-pages).
Letter to FBI Director Mueller.

Background on Anti-Terrorism Information and FBI Interviews

I was a former FBI Special Agent and a Lieutenant Colonel in the US Army Reserve. My FBI credential number was 3437 and my FBI badge number was 790. Between 1978 and 1988, I worked in the FBI's New York Field Office on both the Foreign Counter-Intelligence Division and the Criminal Division.

During the summer of 2001, I met another inmate at this prison by the name of MIAN FAROOQ, NYS DIN # 00A6040. Having served in the Pakistani Air Force, Farooq noted that he flew United Nations missions back in the early 1980s. Recruited by the US CIA, Farooq eventually came to America, secured a position with US Customs Service as an agent and became an American citizen. He has extensive knowledge and background in Pakistani and Afghanistani affairs.

Having developed a friendship during our incarceration, Farooq disclosed to me his background working for the CIA. On the afternoon of September 11, immediately after the World Trade Center and other air attacks, Farooq told me he knew the identity of at least one of the pilots whom he said was a ringleader. That individual he said was MOHAMED ATTA.

This disclosure occurred before any of the news media reported on the alleged perpetrators. Further, on the afternoon of Sep. 11, Farooq added more details about Atta. Farooq stated that he met Mohamed Atta on a few occasions. Once in 1996 while at JFK International Airport, Farooq met Atta who was dressed as an airline pilot. When Farooq asked him what airlines Atta worked for, Atta replied that he operate a Florida-based flight school. Additional information was given to me by Farooq on the terrorist objectives, background and people during that tragic day. This information also contained reference to an "Anthrax" attack.

This information was reported to both the FBI and prison officials by several communications, both in person and in writing.

On October 1, 2001, Farooq told me still more details, identifying people by name and address who supported the Al Qaeda terrorist network. When asked why he did not report this to his former CIA handlers, he said that he does not trust them and wanted to notify the FBI as the proper investigative authority on this matter. Farooq said, since I was a former FBI agent, I could provide him access to the right FBI Anti-Terrorist investigators.

The Big Wedding:

It was not until the day after the first "terrorist alert" that I was finally interviewed on October 12 by two "local" FBI agents from the FBI's Plattsburgh Resident Agency. In a separate letter sent by me to the US Attorney General Ashcroft and to the FBI Director Mueller, I informed them of the improper way the two FBI agents handled my interview. It was clear that they did not want any information and only sought to close this "lead." The interviewing agent was discourteous and abrupt, failed to ask questions or explore details, and clearly was not interested in obtaining any further information. Despite the accurate and credible information I gave these FBI agents, they did not interview Farooq until October 30, the day after the second "terrorist alert."

Rather than conducting a proper interview, these two agents insulted both me and Farooq during Farooq's interview. This made Farooq reluctant to tell them any information. Also, it quickly became apparent to Farooq that these FBI agents did not "do their homework" on him. They did not know anything about Farooq's background. So when he was asked to take a polygraph (lie-detector) test, Farooq decided to decline since he felt that neither FBI agent wanted to pursue this matter.

Interestingly, FBI agent Longerhan told him at the conclusion of the interview, "We know you have more information and can confirm what we were given by Mr. Taus. Please call me when you decide to tell me more." SA Longerhan provided Farooq his FBI business card.

Farooq freely told me about this interview and a previous one conducted by his former CIA handler here at Clinton on October 12, 2001. During his interview with the CIA, Farooq was told to "shut up and say nothing." Farooq originally came forward with terrorist information due to the tragic consequences on September 11. There is no question that CIA knew about Mohamed Atta and others, and their activities, as far back as 1996 and failed to take any action. The FBI Foreign Counter-Intelligence Division either was left-in-the-dark on these matters or failed in their investigative duties to properly follow these leads.

As a result, I have written to Attorney-General Ashcroft, FBI Director Mueller and Homeland Security Chief Ridge in an effort to inform them about this information and the US intelligence services failure to take proper action given the credibility and reliability of Farooq's information.

END NOTES

i   Maj. Gen. Vinod Saighal, *Dealing with Global Terrorism: The Way Forward.* (New Delhi: Sterling Publishers, 2003), 71.

ii   Interview with Kathleen Walters on WPTV-NBC Miami, September 22, 2002.

iii   Official Transcript, White House Press Conference, 5/16/02
http://www.whitehouse.gov/news/releases/2002/05/20020516-13.html

iv   Michael Griffin, *Reaping the Whirlwind: The Taliban Movement in Afghanistan.* (UK: Pluto Press, 2001).

WORKS CITED

Bradley Earl Ayers, *The War That Never Was: An Insider's Account of CIA Covert Operations Against Cuba* (New York: The Bobbs-Merrill Company, Inc., 1976)

Jonathan Beaty and S.C. Gwynne, *The Outlaw Bank: A Wild Ride into the Secret Heart of BCCI* (New York: Random House, 1993)

Ari Ben-Menashe, *Prophets of War: Inside the Secret U.S.-Israeli Arms Network* (New York: Sheridan Square Press, 1992)

William Blum, *Killing Hope: U.S. Military and CIA Interventions Since World War II* (Monroe: Common Courage Press, 1995)

Frank Camper, *The MK/Ultra Secret* (Savannah: Christopher Scott Publishing, 1996)

Ward Churchill and Jim Vander Wall, *Agents of Repression: The FBI's Secret Wars Against the Black Panther Party and the American Indian Movement* (Boston: South End Press, 1990)

Richard A. Clarke, *Against All Enemies: Inside America's War on Terror* (New York: Free Press, 2004)

David Corn, *Blond Ghost: Ted Shackley and the CIA's Crusades* (New York: Simon&Schuster, 1994)

John W. DeCamp, *The Franklin Cover-Up: Child Abuse, Satanism, and Murder in Nebraska* (Lincoln: AWT, 2nd edition 1996)

Yosri Fouda and Nick Fielding, *Masterminds of Terror: The Truth Behind the Most Devastating Attack the World has Ever Seen* (New York: Arcade Publishing, 2003)

Michael Hardt and Antonio Negri, *Empire* (Boston: Harvard University Press, 2001)

J.H. Hatfield, *Fortunate Son: George W. Bush and the*

Making of an American President (New York: Soft Skull Press, 2001)

Daniel Hopsicker, *Barry & 'the Boys': The CIA, the Mob and America's Top Secret History* (Eugene: The Mad Cow Press, 2001)

——————— *Welcome to Terrorland: Mohamed Atta & the 9-11 Cover-up in Florida* (Eugene: The Mad Cow Press, 2004)

Peter Lance, *Cover Up: What the Government is Still Hiding about the War on Terror* (New York: Regan Books, 2004)

Anthony Lappé and Stephen Marshall with Ian Inaba, *True Lies* (New York: A Plume Book, 2004)

Counte de Marenches and David A. Andelman, *The Fourth World War: Diplomacy and Espionage in the Age of Terrorism* (New York: William Morrow & Co.)

Bill Minutaglio, *First Son: George W. Bush and the Bush Family Dynasty* (New York: Times Books, a division of Random House, 1999)

Eustace Mullins, *The Curse of Canaan* (Staunton: Revelation Books, 1987)

Kevin Phillips, *American Dynasty: Aristocracy, Fortune, and the Politics of Deceit in the House of Bush* (New York: Penguin Books, 2004)

Ambrose Evans-Pritchard, *The Secret Life of Bill Clinton: The Unreported Stories* (Washington D.C.: Regenery Publishing, Inc., 1997)

Justin Raimondo, *The Terror Enigma: 9/11 and the Israeli Connection* (New York: iUniverse, Inc., 2003)

Dave Ratcliffe, ed. and others, *American Airlines #77 Hit the Pentagon on 9/11/01: Eyewitness Statements and Pictures* (San Francisco: self-published, 2003)

Michael C. Ruppert, *Crossing the Rubicon: The Decline of the American Empire at the End of the Age of Oil* (Canada: New Society Publishers, 2004)

George Stephanopoulos, *All Too Human* (Boston: Back Bay Books, 2000)

Major General Vinod Saighal, *Dealing with Global Terrorism: The Way Forward* (New Delhi: Sterling Publishers Private Limited, 2003)

Claire Sterling, *Thieves' World: The Threat of the New*

Global Network of Organized Crime (New York: Simon&Schuster, 1994)

M. Wesley Swearingen, *FBI Secrets: An Agent's Exposé* (Boston: South End Press, 1995)

Paul Thompson, *The Terror Timeline: Year by Year, Day by Day, Minute by Minute; A Comprehensive Chronicle of the Road to 9/11-and America's Response* (New York: Regan Books, 2004)

Craig Unger, *House of Bush, House of Saud: The Secret Relationship between the World's Two Most Powerful Dynasties* (New York: Scribner, 2004)

Mary Anne Weaver, *A Portrait of Egypt: A Journey Through the World of Militant Islam,* (New York: Farrar, Straus and Giroux revised edition 2000)

The National Commission on Terrorist Attacks Upon the United States, *The 9/11 Commission Report* (New York: W.W. Norton & Company, 2004)

INDEX

Note: "f" following page number indicates photograph
"n" following page numbers refers to footnotes.

A

C

The Big Wedding:

G

H

U

V

W

Y

Z

THANKS

Thanks be to God.

Thanks to Allan Duncan for research. Thanks, Holley Anderson for your faith in this project. Special Thanks to Anthony Lappé and Guerrilla News Network who originally commissioned material that later appeared in Chapters 5 and 8. Thanks to Paul Thompson for reading the galley and offerering suggestions. Thanks to my "SEC Contact" for tips and clippings.

Thanks to Everyone at INN World Report television, Edith Updike at *Long Island Press,* and Alexander Zaitchik at *New York Press.* Thanks to Melissa Johnson, at the *San Marcos University Star.* Some of the material in Chapters 3, 6 and 10 first appeared in the *Long Island Press, New York Press* and *San Marcos University Star,* respectively.

Thank you, Emmy Gilbert and Alex Crowley. Thanks, Kurt Brechter for all the Satyagraha. Thanks for the book-work: Alexis Wichowski, Rebecca DeRosa, Larry Eldridge, Melissa Johnson, Rachel Simons & Louisa McMurray. BIG Thanks, Aaron and Gabriel at SCB Book Distributors.

Thanks for the speaking engagements: 9/11 International Inquiry (especially Carol Brouillet) and New York 9/11 Truth (especially Nick Levis and Les Jamieson).

THANKS TO EVERYONE WHO SUBMITTED TO QUESTIONING AND GRANTED ME AN INTERVIEW:

Brad Ayers, Steve Barborini, Richard Ben-Veniste, Phil Berg, Javid Burki, John H. Clarke, Mitchell Cohen, Connie Cook Smith, Derek Davidson, Lisa DeWitt, David Emory, Kenneth Feinberg, James Fetzer, Ph.D., Jim Funck, Randy Glass, Jamey Hecht, Ph.D., Kyle Hence, Tom Henry, Ann Marie Hicks, Daniel Hopsicker, Adam Hurter, Kezia Jauron, John Judge, Michael Kane, Johanna Klein, Patrick Knowlton, Arnie Kruithof, Ellen Mariani, John Mintz, Colin Moynihan, Greg Palast, Al Rogers, Coleen Rowley, Mike Ruppert, Fred Schlange, Penny Schoner, Peter Dale Scott, Ph.D., Richard Taus, Demitria Monde Thraam, Hugh Turley, Jon Vincent, Delmart Vreeland, Ambassador Leo Wanta, and Evan West.

PEACE BE WITH ALL OF YOU.